The LAST Musketeer

FANTAGRAPHICS BOOKS

by Jason
Colored by Hubert

FANTAGRAPHICS BOOKS • 7563 Lake City Way NE • Seattle WA 98115

DESIGNED by Jason and Covey | PRODUCTION by Paul Baresh and Jacob Covey
EDITED & TRANSLATED by Kim Thompson | PUBLISHED by Gary Groth and Kim Thompson

Special thanks to Jérôme at Editions de Tournon – Carabas.

To receive a free catalog of comics, call
1-800-657-1100 or write us at the above address.

Distributed in the U.S. by W.W. Norton and Company, Inc. (212-354-5500) • Distributed in Canada by Raincoast Books (800-663-5714) • Distributed in the United Kingdom by Turnaround Distribution (208-829-3009)

Visit the website for Jippi, who originally publishes Jason's work, at www.jippicomics.com
Visit the website for The Beguiling, where Jason's original artwork can be purchased: www.beguiling.com
Visit the Fantagraphics website, just because: www.fantagraphics.com

---

FIRST PRINTING: December 2007 • ISBN: 978-1-56097-889-3 • PRINTED in Singapore

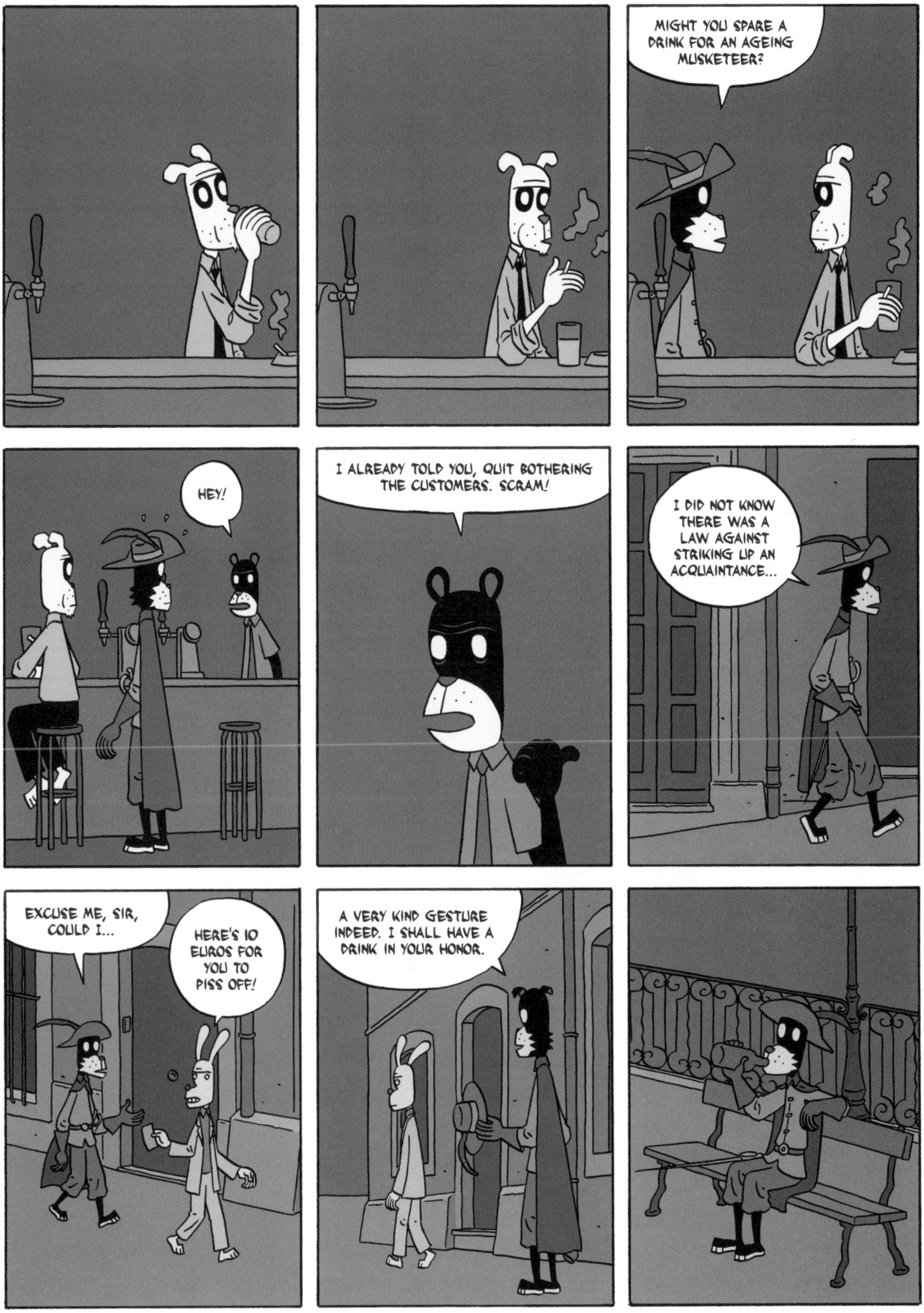
MIGHT YOU SPARE A DRINK FOR AN AGEING MUSKETEER?
HEY!
I ALREADY TOLD YOU, QUIT BOTHERING THE CUSTOMERS. SCRAM!
I DID NOT KNOW THERE WAS A LAW AGAINST STRIKING UP AN ACQUAINTANCE...
EXCUSE ME, SIR, COULD I...
HERE'S 10 EUROS FOR YOU TO PISS OFF!
A VERY KIND GESTURE INDEED. I SHALL HAVE A DRINK IN YOUR HONOR.

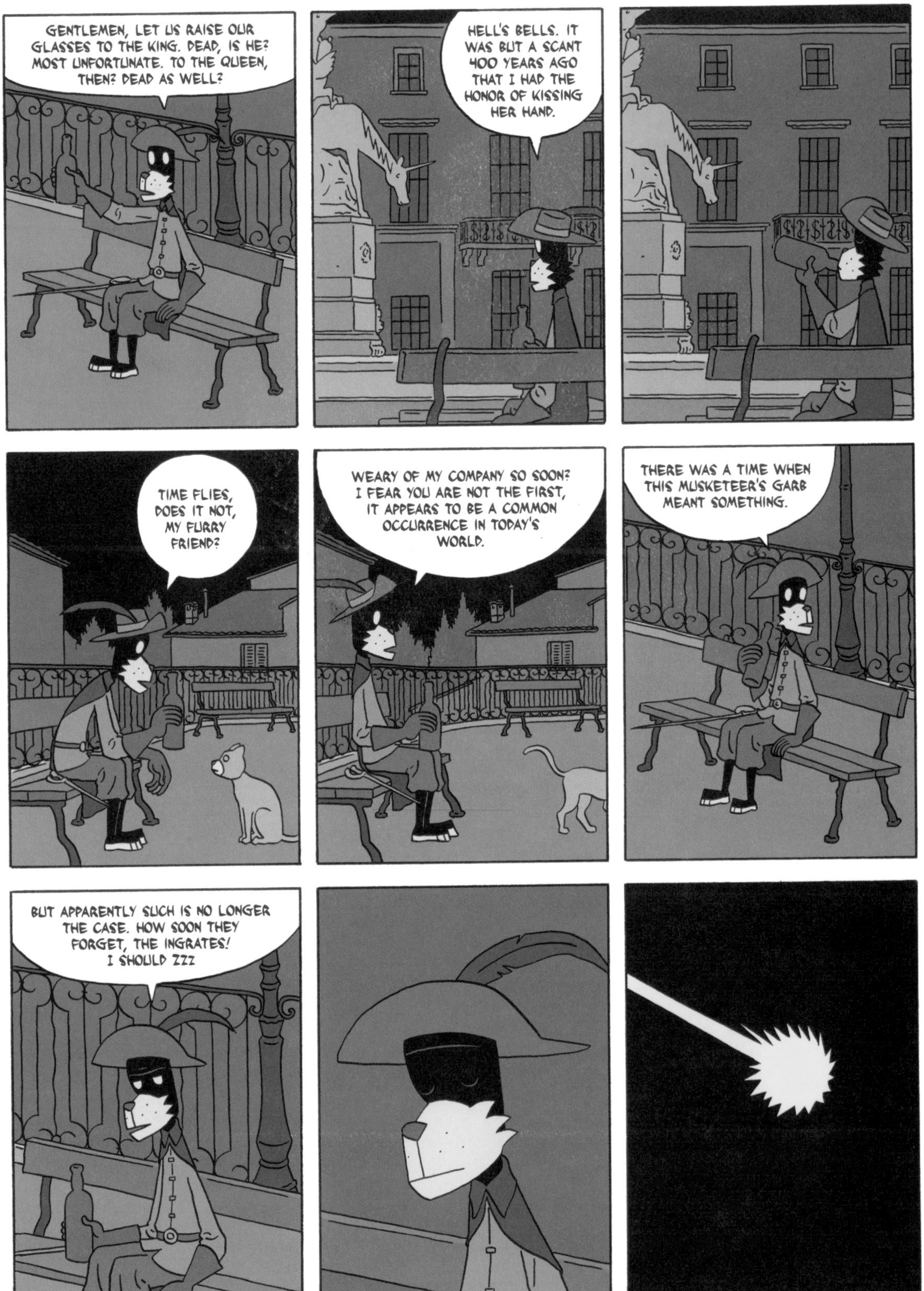
GENTLEMEN, LET US RAISE OUR GLASSES TO THE KING. DEAD, IS HE? MOST UNFORTUNATE. TO THE QUEEN, THEN? DEAD AS WELL?
HELL'S BELLS. IT WAS BUT A SCANT 400 YEARS AGO THAT I HAD THE HONOR OF KISSING HER HAND.
TIME FLIES, DOES IT NOT, MY FURRY FRIEND?
WEARY OF MY COMPANY SO SOON? I FEAR YOU ARE NOT THE FIRST, IT APPEARS TO BE A COMMON OCCURRENCE IN TODAY'S WORLD.
THERE WAS A TIME WHEN THIS MUSKETEER'S GARB MEANT SOMETHING.
BUT APPARENTLY SUCH IS NO LONGER THE CASE. HOW SOON THEY FORGET, THE INGRATES! I SHOULD ZZZ

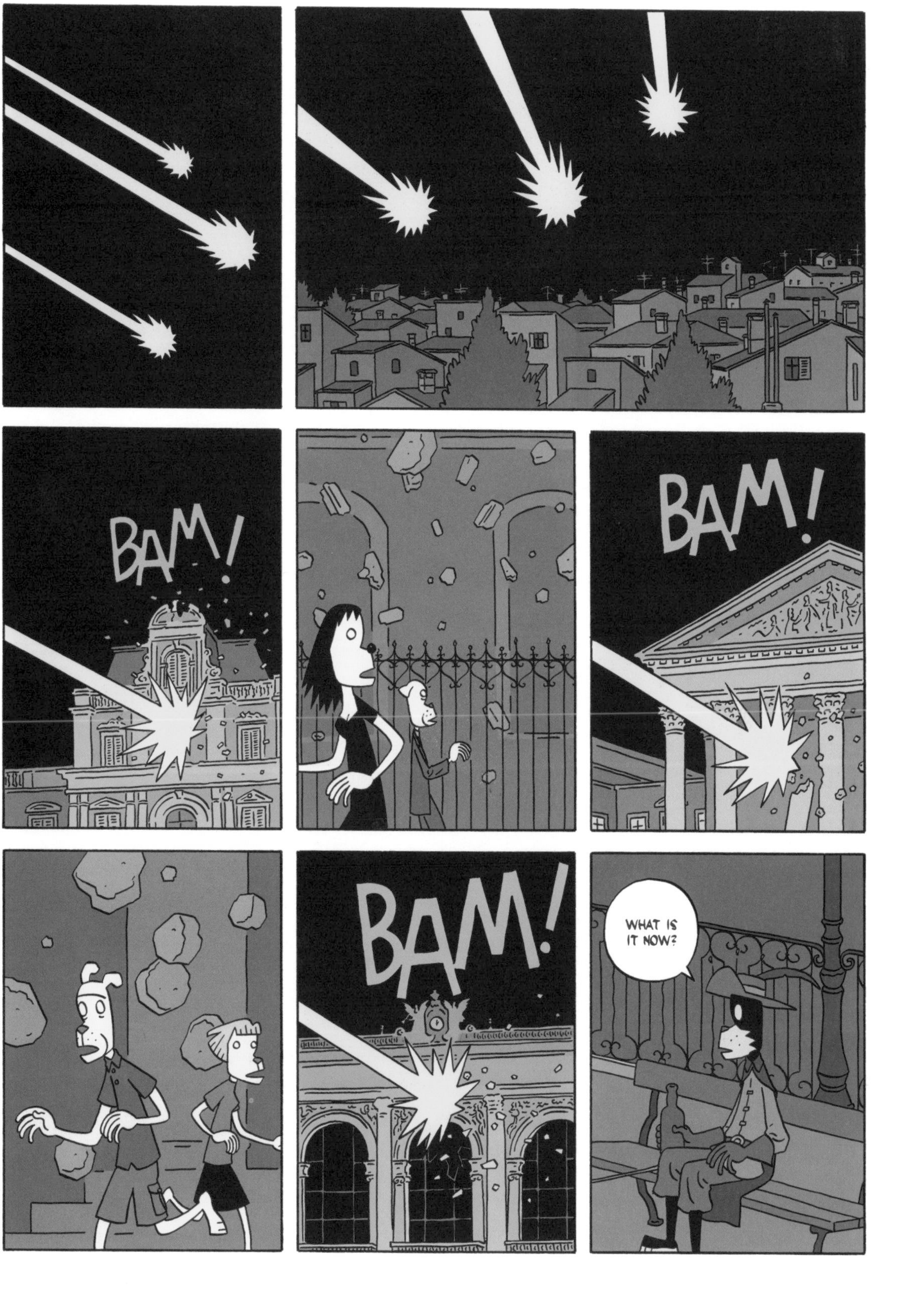
BAM!
BAM!
BAM!
WHAT IS IT NOW?

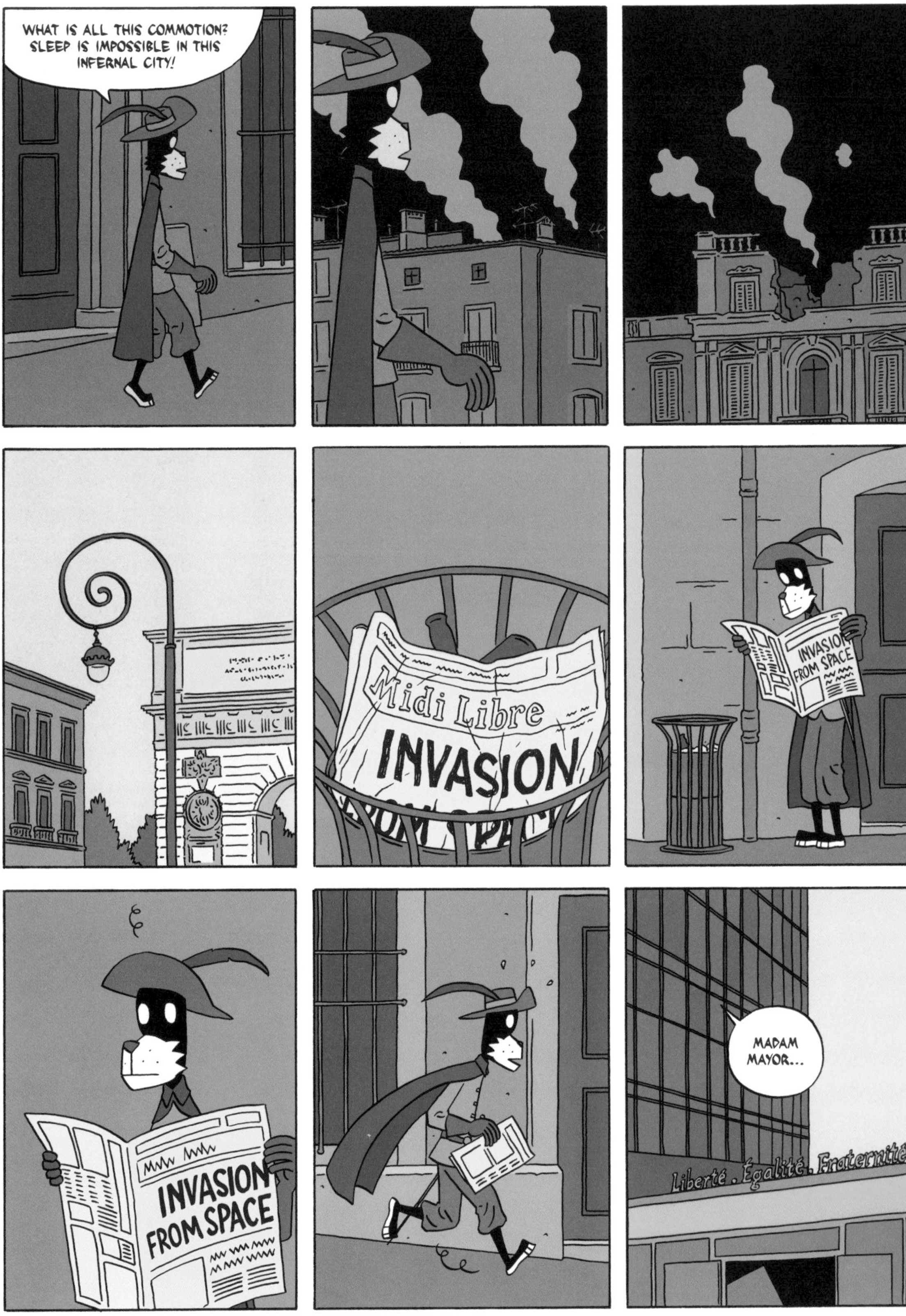

WHAT IS ALL THIS COMMOTION? SLEEP IS IMPOSSIBLE IN THIS INFERNAL CITY!
Midi Libre
INVASION
INVASION FROM SPACE
INVASION FROM SPACE
MADAM MAYOR...
Liberté . Égalité . Fraternité

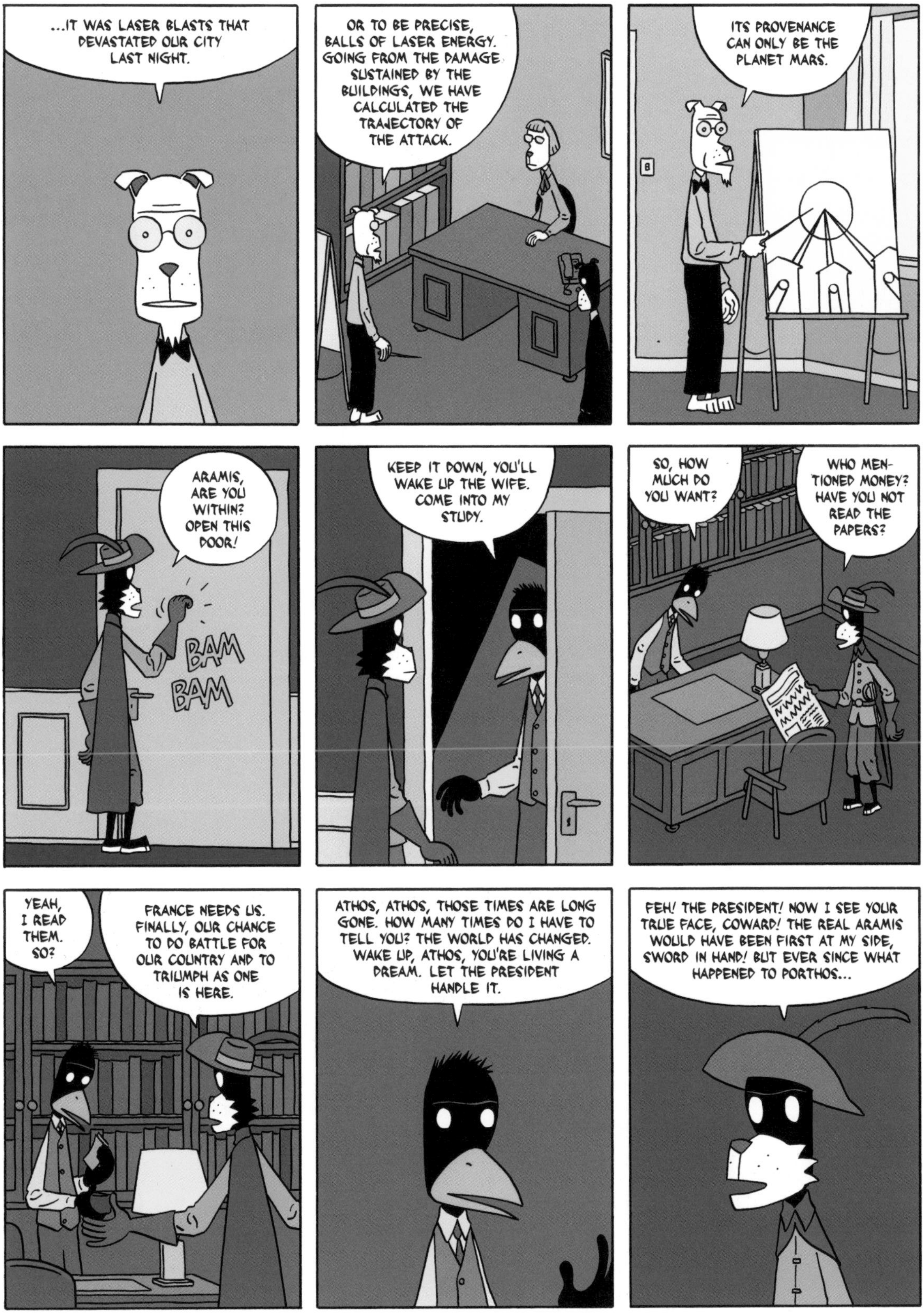
...IT WAS LASER BLASTS THAT DEVASTATED OUR CITY LAST NIGHT.
OR TO BE PRECISE, BALLS OF LASER ENERGY. GOING FROM THE DAMAGE SUSTAINED BY THE BUILDINGS, WE HAVE CALCULATED THE TRAJECTORY OF THE ATTACK.
ITS PROVENANCE CAN ONLY BE THE PLANET MARS.
ARAMIS, ARE YOU WITHIN? OPEN THIS DOOR!
BAM BAM
KEEP IT DOWN, YOU'LL WAKE UP THE WIFE. COME INTO MY STUDY.
SO, HOW MUCH DO YOU WANT?
WHO MENTIONED MONEY? HAVE YOU NOT READ THE PAPERS?
YEAH, I READ THEM. SO?
FRANCE NEEDS US. FINALLY, OUR CHANCE TO DO BATTLE FOR OUR COUNTRY AND TO TRIUMPH AS ONE IS HERE.
ATHOS, ATHOS, THOSE TIMES ARE LONG GONE. HOW MANY TIMES DO I HAVE TO TELL YOU? THE WORLD HAS CHANGED. WAKE UP, ATHOS, YOU'RE LIVING A DREAM. LET THE PRESIDENT HANDLE IT.
FEH! THE PRESIDENT! NOW I SEE YOUR TRUE FACE, COWARD! THE REAL ARAMIS WOULD HAVE BEEN FIRST AT MY SIDE, SWORD IN HAND! BUT EVER SINCE WHAT HAPPENED TO PORTHOS...

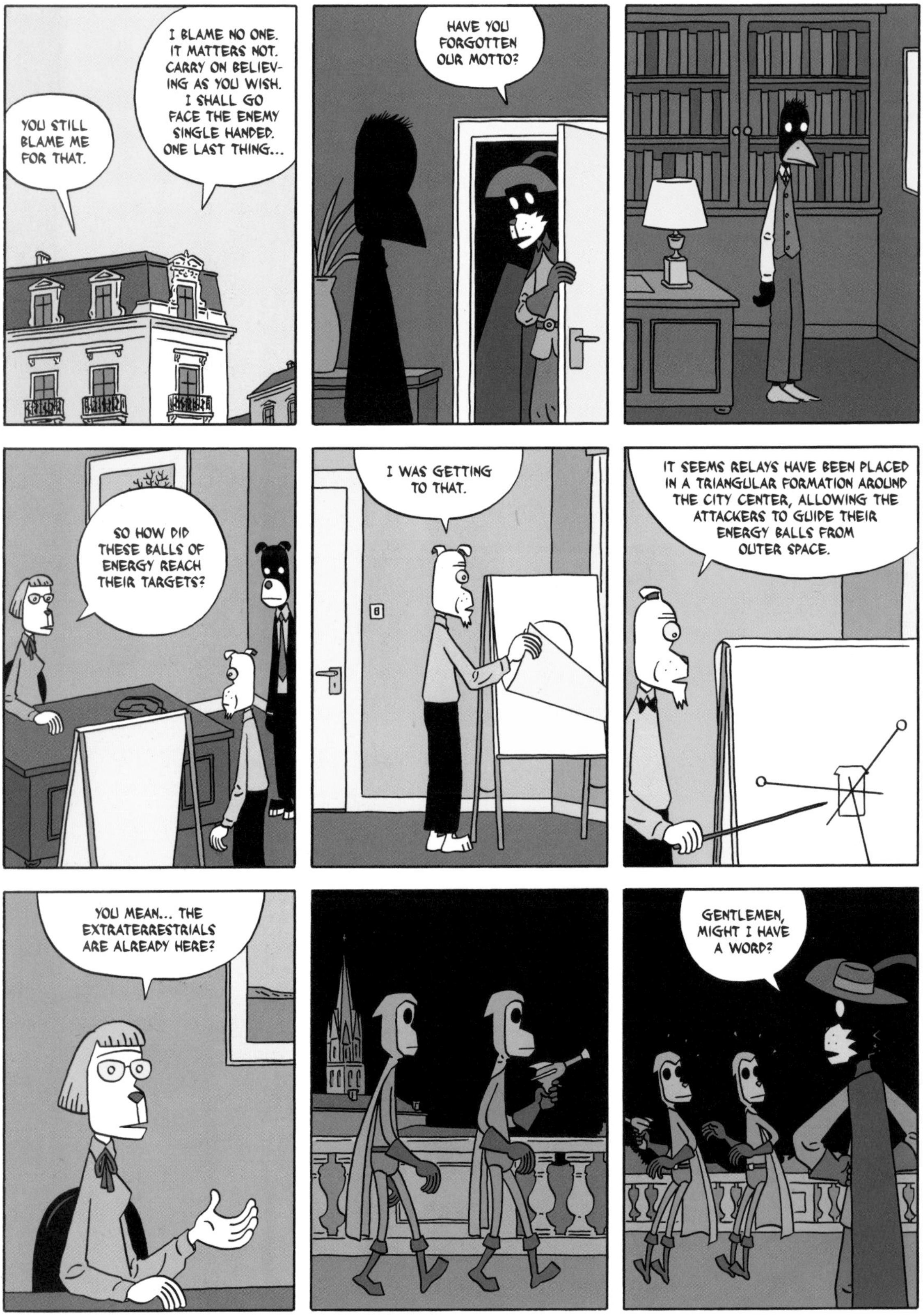
YOU STILL BLAME ME FOR THAT.
I BLAME NO ONE. IT MATTERS NOT. CARRY ON BELIEVING AS YOU WISH. I SHALL GO FACE THE ENEMY SINGLE HANDED. ONE LAST THING...
HAVE YOU FORGOTTEN OUR MOTTO?
SO HOW DID THESE BALLS OF ENERGY REACH THEIR TARGETS?
I WAS GETTING TO THAT.
IT SEEMS RELAYS HAVE BEEN PLACED IN A TRIANGULAR FORMATION AROUND THE CITY CENTER, ALLOWING THE ATTACKERS TO GUIDE THEIR ENERGY BALLS FROM OUTER SPACE.
YOU MEAN... THE EXTRATERRESTRIALS ARE ALREADY HERE?
GENTLEMEN, MIGHT I HAVE A WORD?

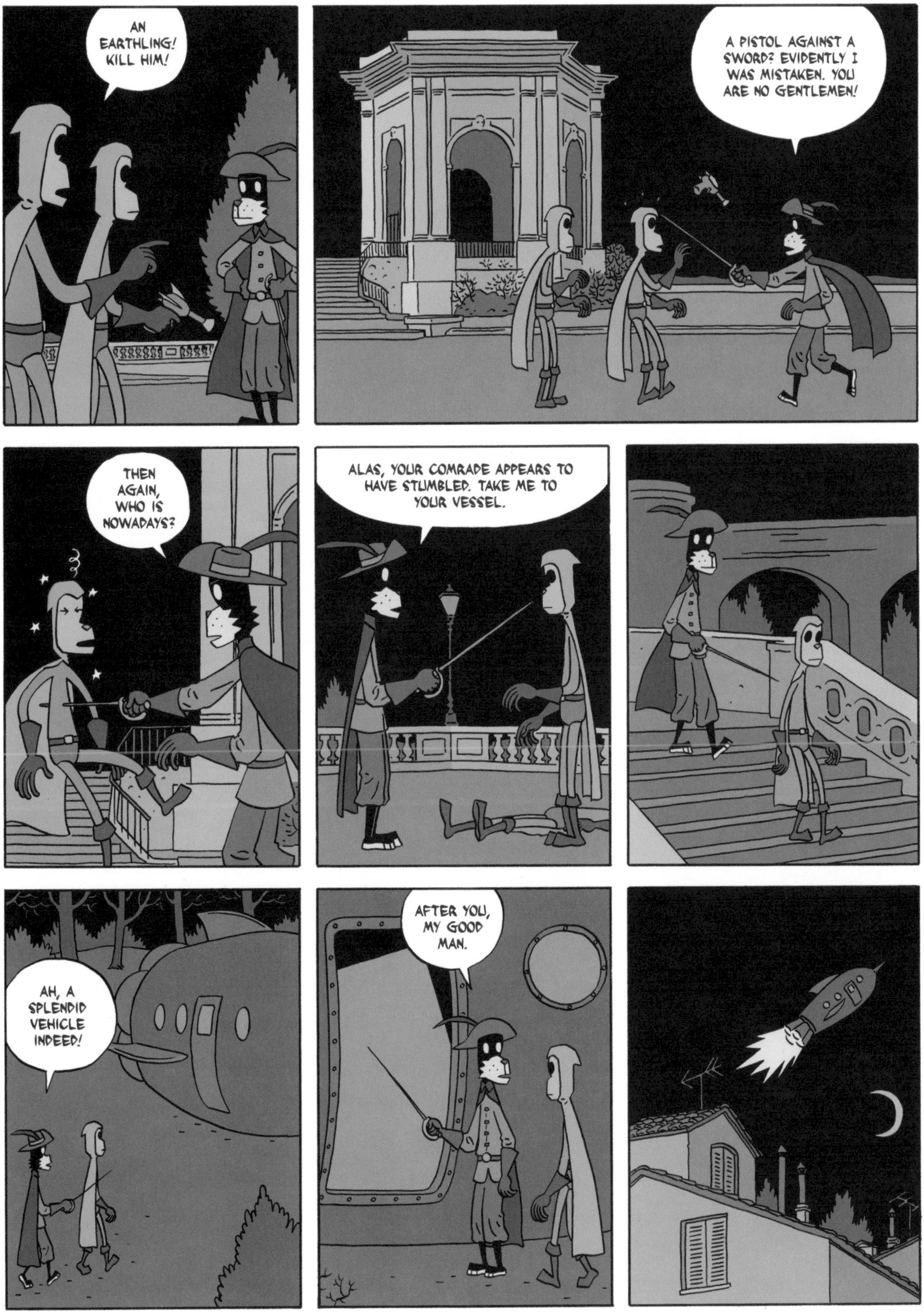
AN EARTHLING! KILL HIM!
A PISTOL AGAINST A SWORD? EVIDENTLY I WAS MISTAKEN. YOU ARE NO GENTLEMEN!
THEN AGAIN, WHO IS NOWADAYS?
ALAS, YOUR COMRADE APPEARS TO HAVE STUMBLED. TAKE ME TO YOUR VESSEL.
AH, A SPLENDID VEHICLE INDEED!
AFTER YOU, MY GOOD MAN.

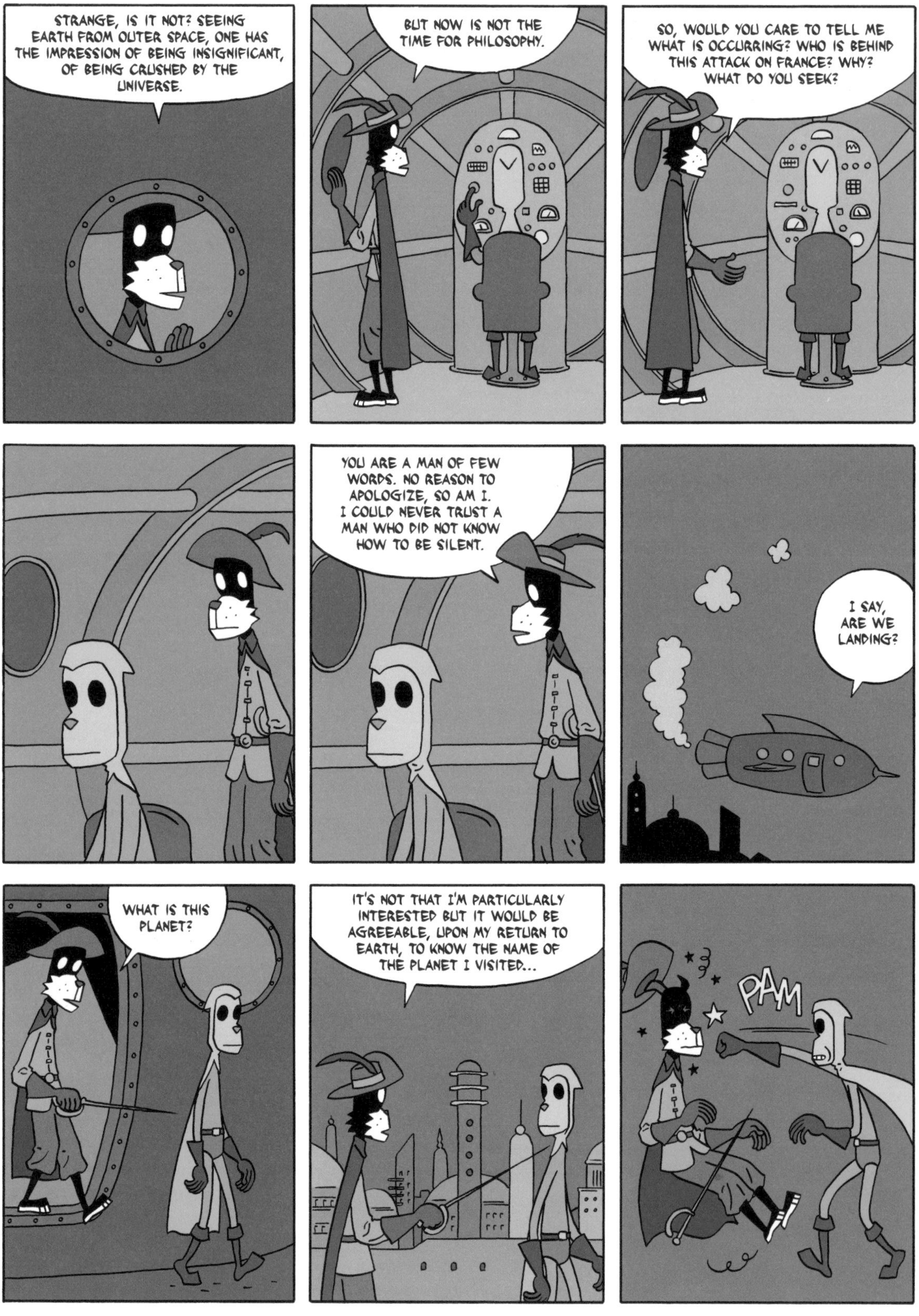
STRANGE, IS IT NOT? SEEING EARTH FROM OUTER SPACE, ONE HAS THE IMPRESSION OF BEING INSIGNIFICANT, OF BEING CRUSHED BY THE UNIVERSE.
BUT NOW IS NOT THE TIME FOR PHILOSOPHY.
SO, WOULD YOU CARE TO TELL ME WHAT IS OCCURRING? WHO IS BEHIND THIS ATTACK ON FRANCE? WHY? WHAT DO YOU SEEK?
YOU ARE A MAN OF FEW WORDS. NO REASON TO APOLOGIZE, SO AM I. I COULD NEVER TRUST A MAN WHO DID NOT KNOW HOW TO BE SILENT.
I SAY, ARE WE LANDING?
WHAT IS THIS PLANET?
IT'S NOT THAT I'M PARTICULARLY INTERESTED BUT IT WOULD BE AGREEABLE, UPON MY RETURN TO EARTH, TO KNOW THE NAME OF THE PLANET I VISITED...
PAM

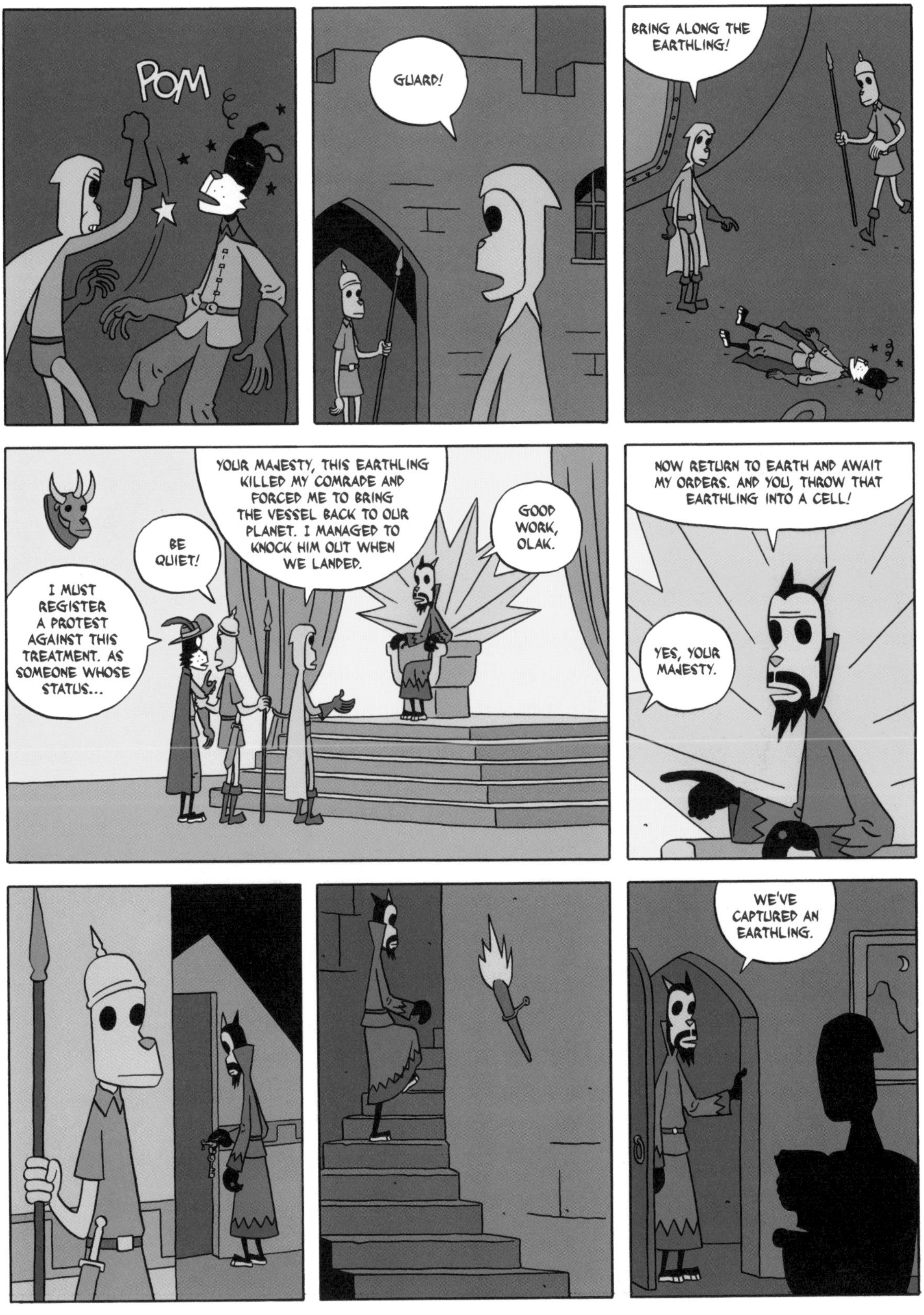
POM
GUARD!
BRING ALONG THE EARTHLING!
I MUST REGISTER A PROTEST AGAINST THIS TREATMENT. AS SOMEONE WHOSE STATUS...
BE QUIET!
YOUR MAJESTY, THIS EARTHLING KILLED MY COMRADE AND FORCED ME TO BRING THE VESSEL BACK TO OUR PLANET. I MANAGED TO KNOCK HIM OUT WHEN WE LANDED.
GOOD WORK, OLAK.
NOW RETURN TO EARTH AND AWAIT MY ORDERS. AND YOU, THROW THAT EARTHLING INTO A CELL!
YES, YOUR MAJESTY.
WE'VE CAPTURED AN EARTHLING.

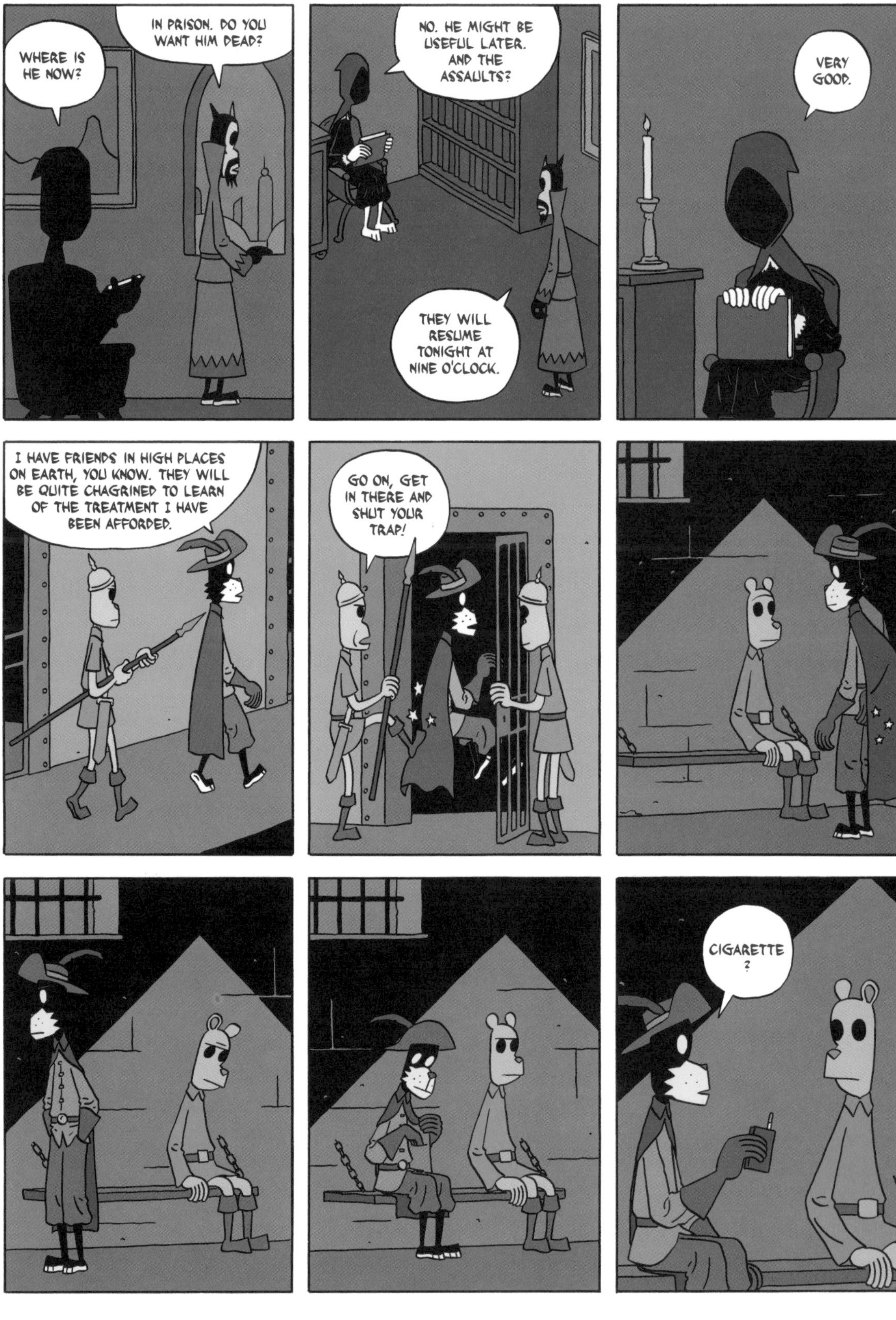
WHERE IS HE NOW?
IN PRISON. DO YOU WANT HIM DEAD?
NO. HE MIGHT BE USEFUL LATER. AND THE ASSAULTS?
THEY WILL RESUME TONIGHT AT NINE O'CLOCK.
VERY GOOD.
I HAVE FRIENDS IN HIGH PLACES ON EARTH, YOU KNOW. THEY WILL BE QUITE CHAGRINED TO LEARN OF THE TREATMENT I HAVE BEEN AFFORDED.
GO ON, GET IN THERE AND SHUT YOUR TRAP!
CIGARETTE ?

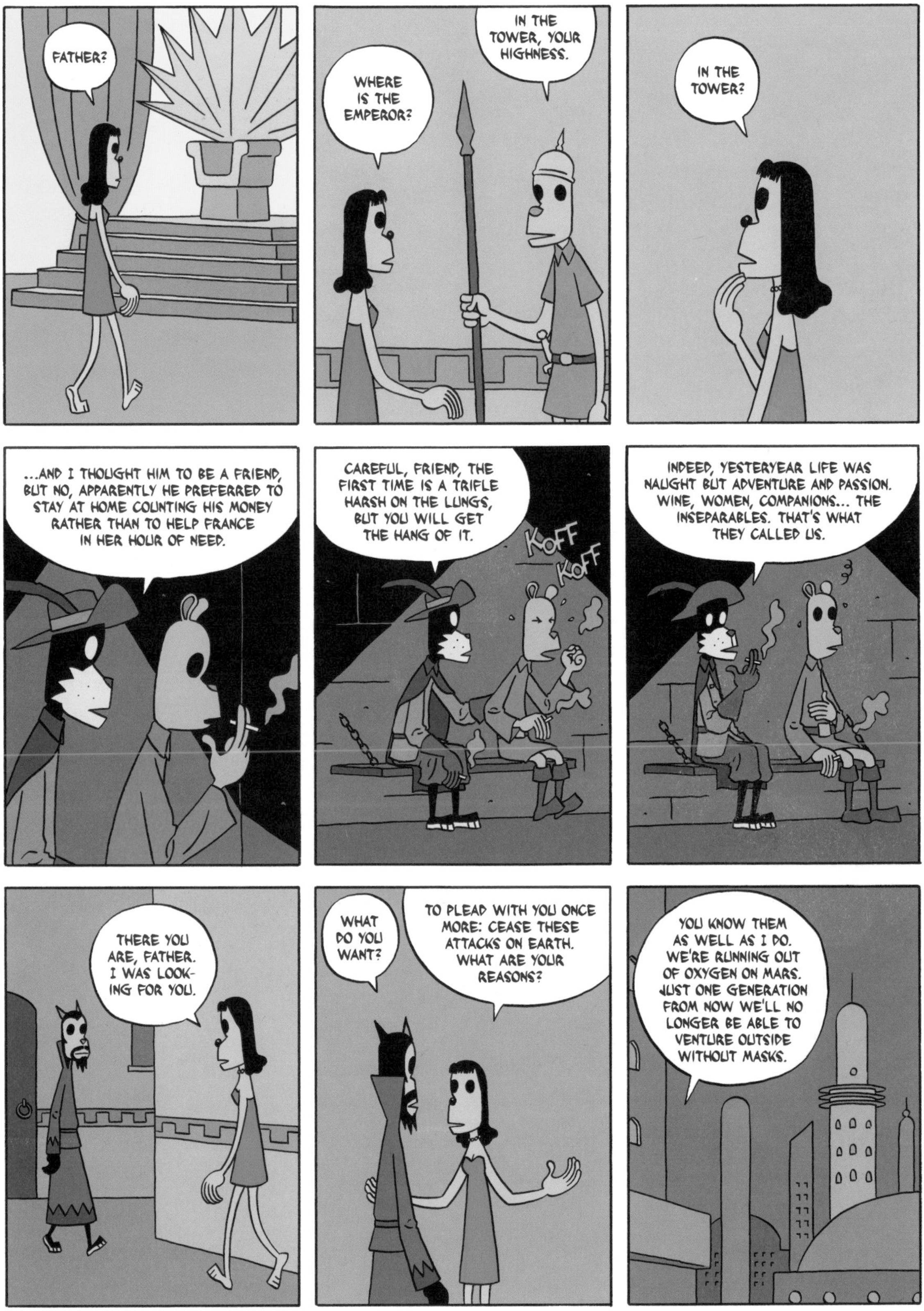
FATHER?
WHERE IS THE EMPEROR?
IN THE TOWER, YOUR HIGHNESS.
IN THE TOWER?
...AND I THOUGHT HIM TO BE A FRIEND, BUT NO, APPARENTLY HE PREFERRED TO STAY AT HOME COUNTING HIS MONEY RATHER THAN TO HELP FRANCE IN HER HOUR OF NEED.
CAREFUL, FRIEND, THE FIRST TIME IS A TRIFLE HARSH ON THE LUNGS, BUT YOU WILL GET THE HANG OF IT.
KOFF KOFF
INDEED, YESTERYEAR LIFE WAS NAUGHT BUT ADVENTURE AND PASSION. WINE, WOMEN, COMPANIONS... THE INSEPARABLES. THAT'S WHAT THEY CALLED US.
THERE YOU ARE, FATHER. I WAS LOOKING FOR YOU.
WHAT DO YOU WANT?
TO PLEAD WITH YOU ONCE MORE: CEASE THESE ATTACKS ON EARTH. WHAT ARE YOUR REASONS?
YOU KNOW THEM AS WELL AS I DO. WE'RE RUNNING OUT OF OXYGEN ON MARS. JUST ONE GENERATION FROM NOW WE'LL NO LONGER BE ABLE TO VENTURE OUTSIDE WITHOUT MASKS.

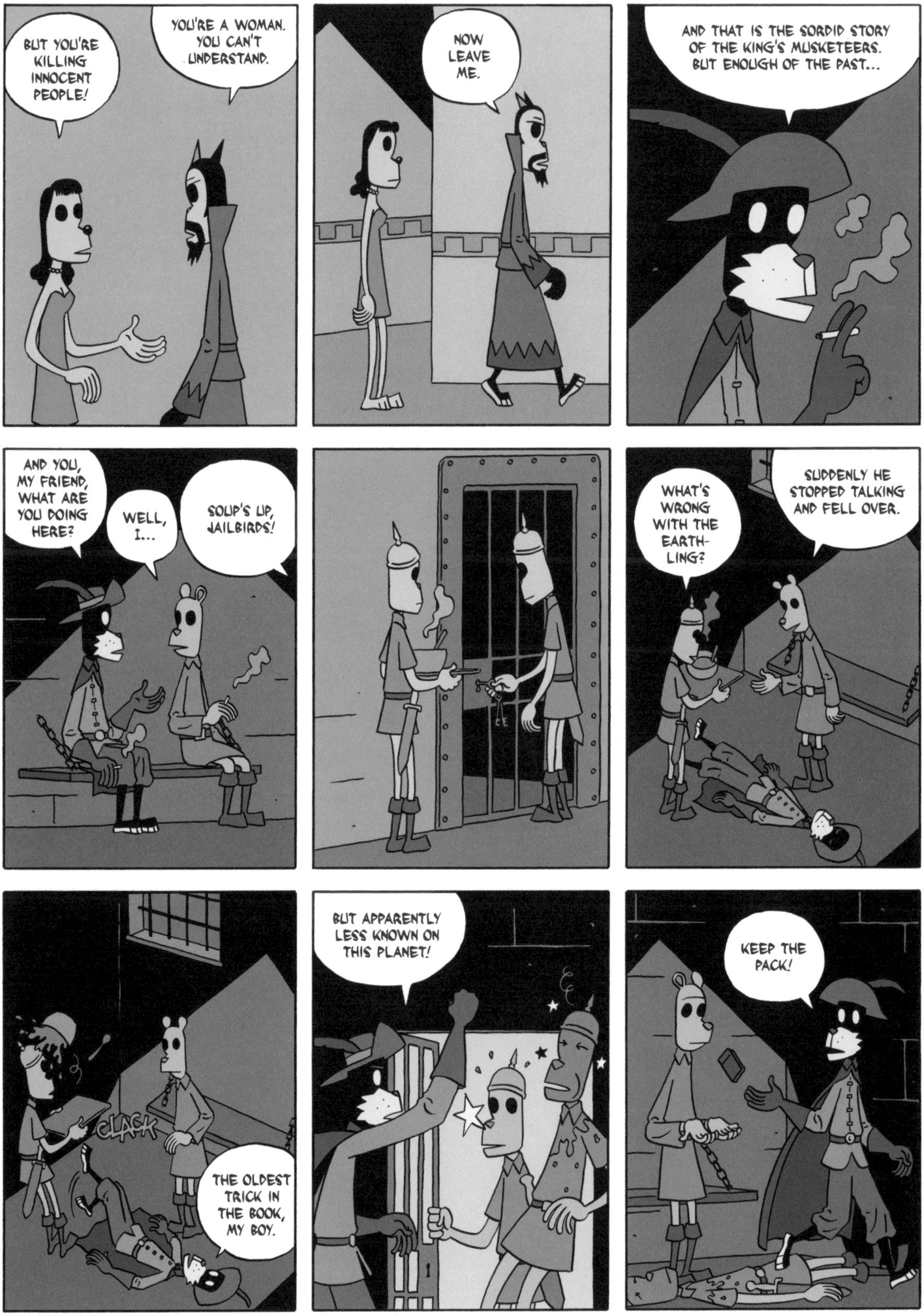
BUT YOU'RE KILLING INNOCENT PEOPLE!
YOU'RE A WOMAN. YOU CAN'T UNDERSTAND.
NOW LEAVE ME.
AND THAT IS THE SORDID STORY OF THE KING'S MUSKETEERS. BUT ENOUGH OF THE PAST...
AND YOU, MY FRIEND, WHAT ARE YOU DOING HERE?
WELL, I...
SOUP'S UP, JAILBIRDS!
WHAT'S WRONG WITH THE EARTH-LING?
SUDDENLY HE STOPPED TALKING AND FELL OVER.
CLACK
THE OLDEST TRICK IN THE BOOK, MY BOY.
BUT APPARENTLY LESS KNOWN ON THIS PLANET!
KEEP THE PACK!

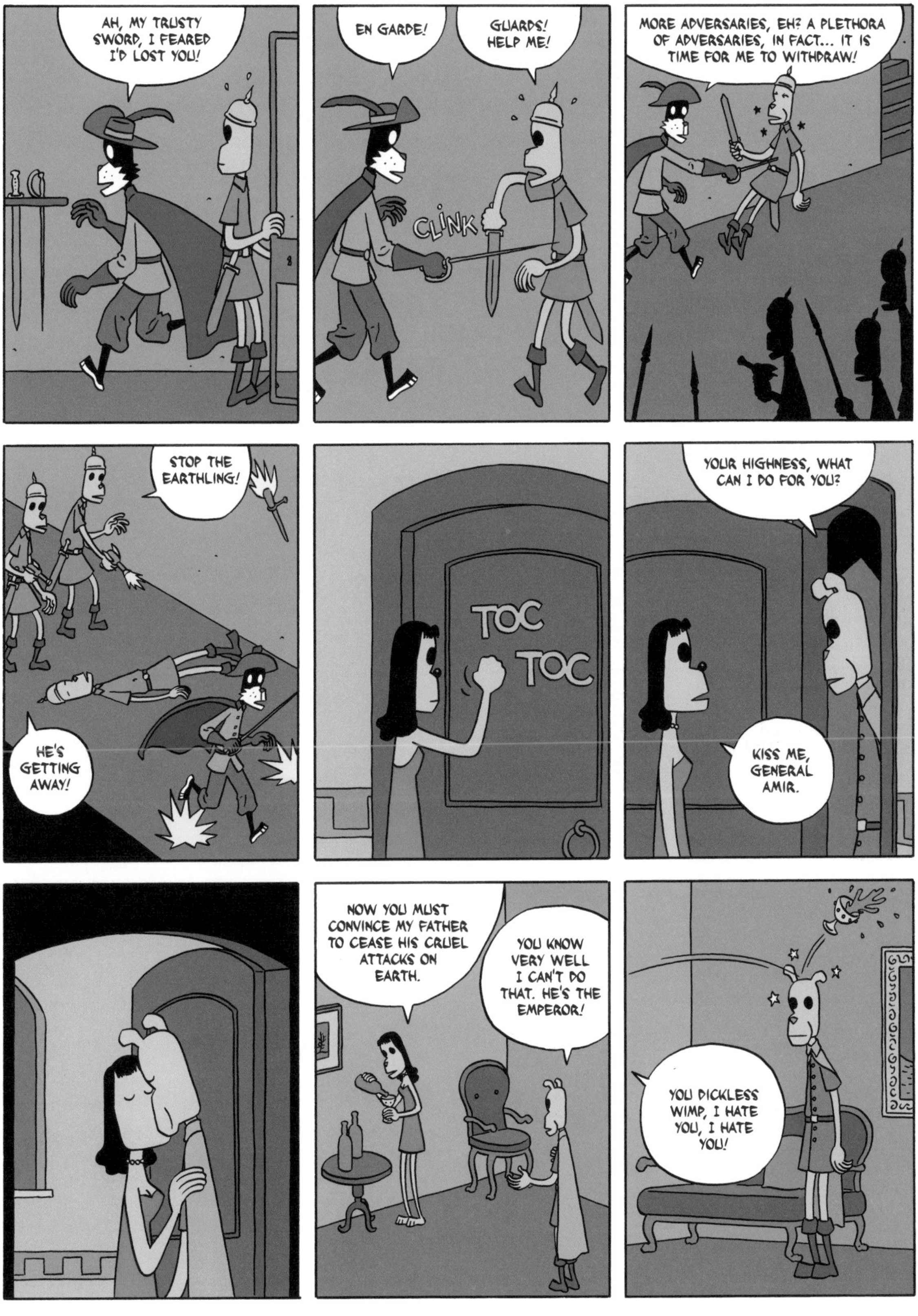
AH, MY TRUSTY SWORD, I FEARED I'D LOST YOU!
EN GARDE!
GUARDS! HELP ME!
CLINK
MORE ADVERSARIES, EH? A PLETHORA OF ADVERSARIES, IN FACT... IT IS TIME FOR ME TO WITHDRAW!
STOP THE EARTHLING!
HE'S GETTING AWAY!
TOC
TOC
YOUR HIGHNESS, WHAT CAN I DO FOR YOU?
KISS ME, GENERAL AMIR.
NOW YOU MUST CONVINCE MY FATHER TO CEASE HIS CRUEL ATTACKS ON EARTH.
YOU KNOW VERY WELL I CAN'T DO THAT. HE'S THE EMPEROR!
YOU DICKLESS WIMP, I HATE YOU, I HATE YOU!

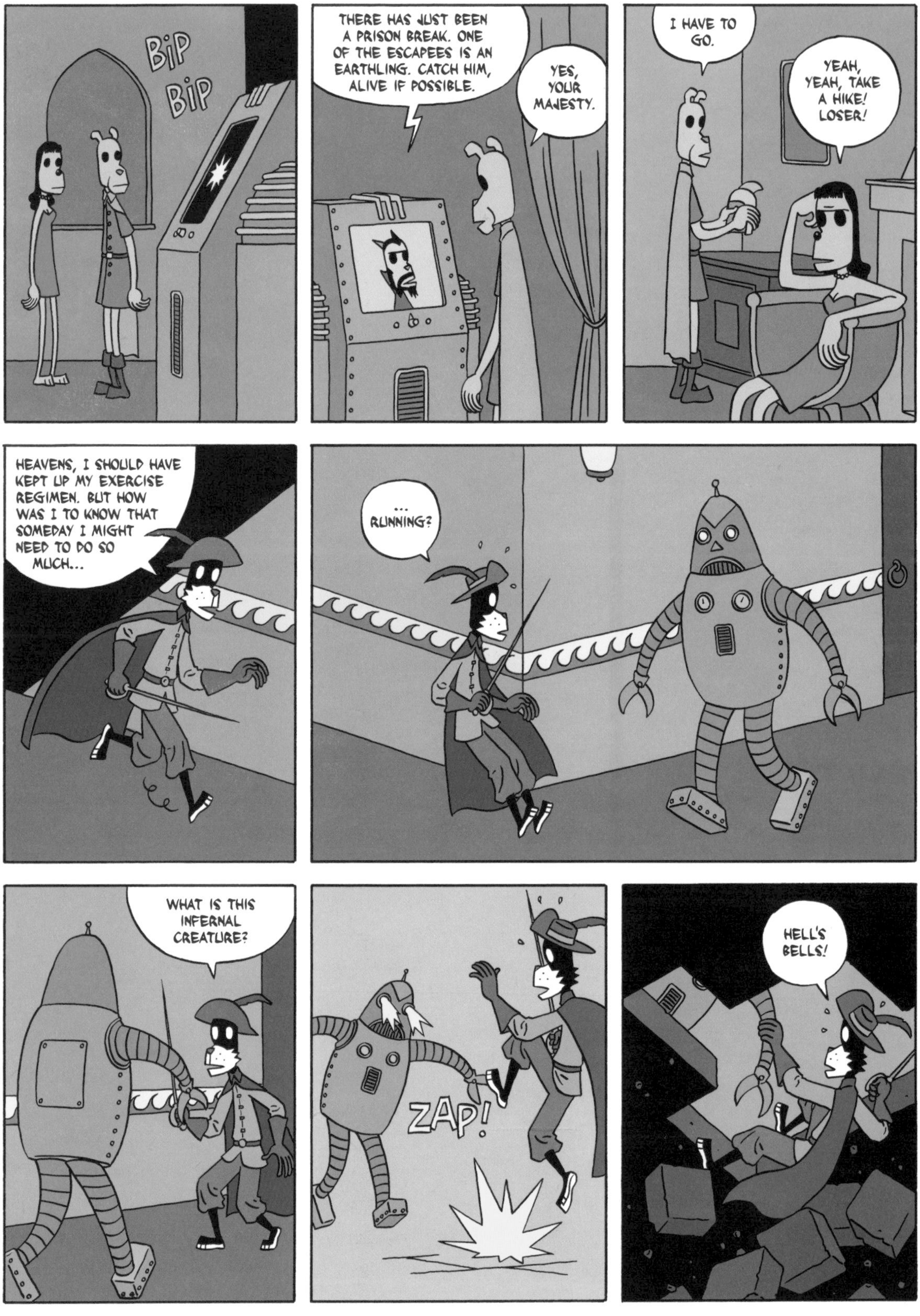
BIP BIP
THERE HAS JUST BEEN A PRISON BREAK. ONE OF THE ESCAPEES IS AN EARTHLING. CATCH HIM, ALIVE IF POSSIBLE.
YES, YOUR MAJESTY.
I HAVE TO GO.
YEAH, YEAH, TAKE A HIKE! LOSER!
HEAVENS, I SHOULD HAVE KEPT UP MY EXERCISE REGIMEN. BUT HOW WAS I TO KNOW THAT SOMEDAY I MIGHT NEED TO DO SO MUCH...
... RUNNING?
WHAT IS THIS INFERNAL CREATURE?
ZAP!
HELL'S BELLS!

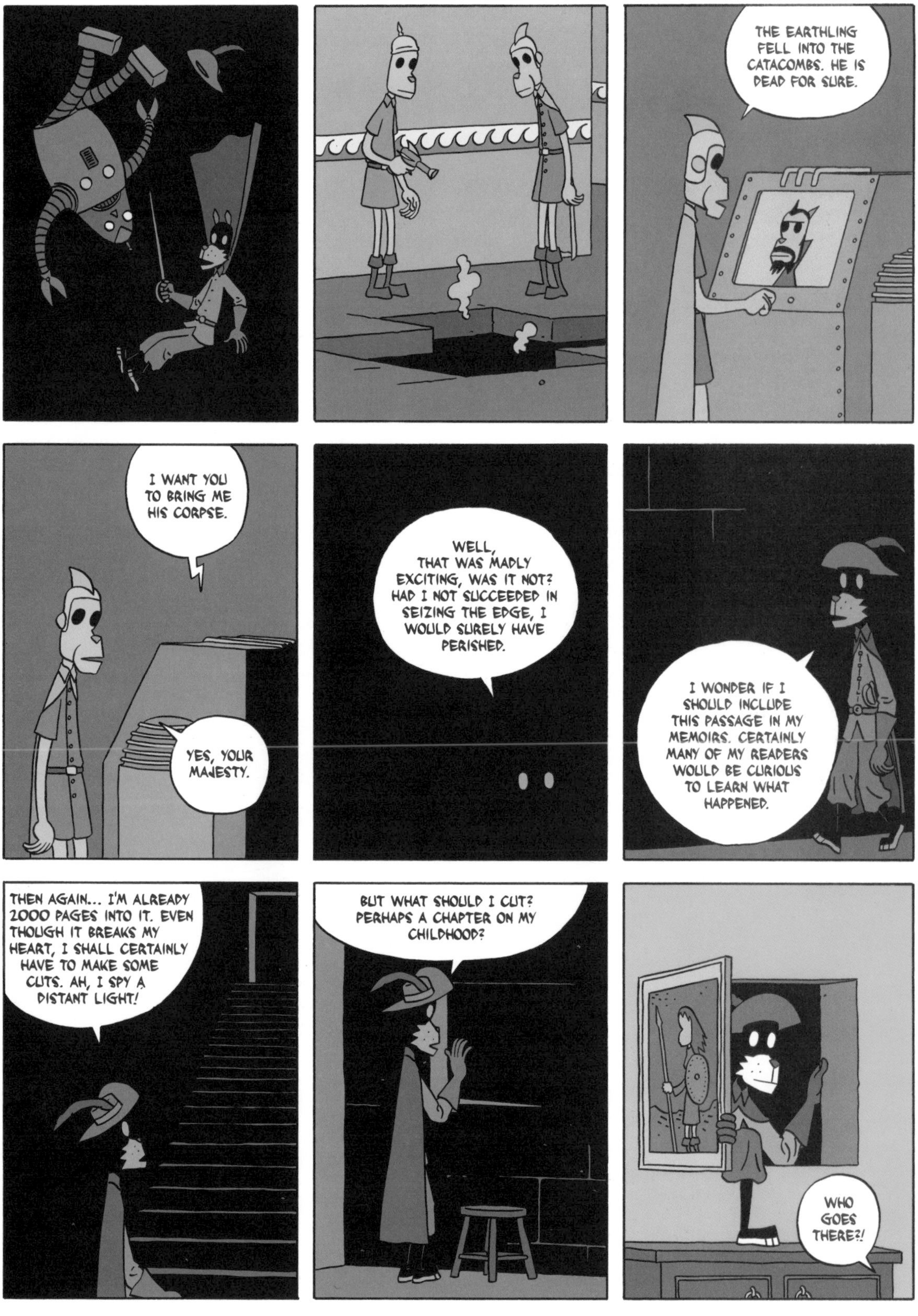
THE EARTHLING FELL INTO THE CATACOMBS. HE IS DEAD FOR SURE.
I WANT YOU TO BRING ME HIS CORPSE.
YES, YOUR MAJESTY.
WELL, THAT WAS MADLY EXCITING, WAS IT NOT? HAD I NOT SUCCEEDED IN SEIZING THE EDGE, I WOULD SURELY HAVE PERISHED.
I WONDER IF I SHOULD INCLUDE THIS PASSAGE IN MY MEMOIRS. CERTAINLY MANY OF MY READERS WOULD BE CURIOUS TO LEARN WHAT HAPPENED.
THEN AGAIN... I'M ALREADY 2000 PAGES INTO IT. EVEN THOUGH IT BREAKS MY HEART, I SHALL CERTAINLY HAVE TO MAKE SOME CUTS. AH, I SPY A DISTANT LIGHT!
BUT WHAT SHOULD I CUT? PERHAPS A CHAPTER ON MY CHILDHOOD?
WHO GOES THERE?!

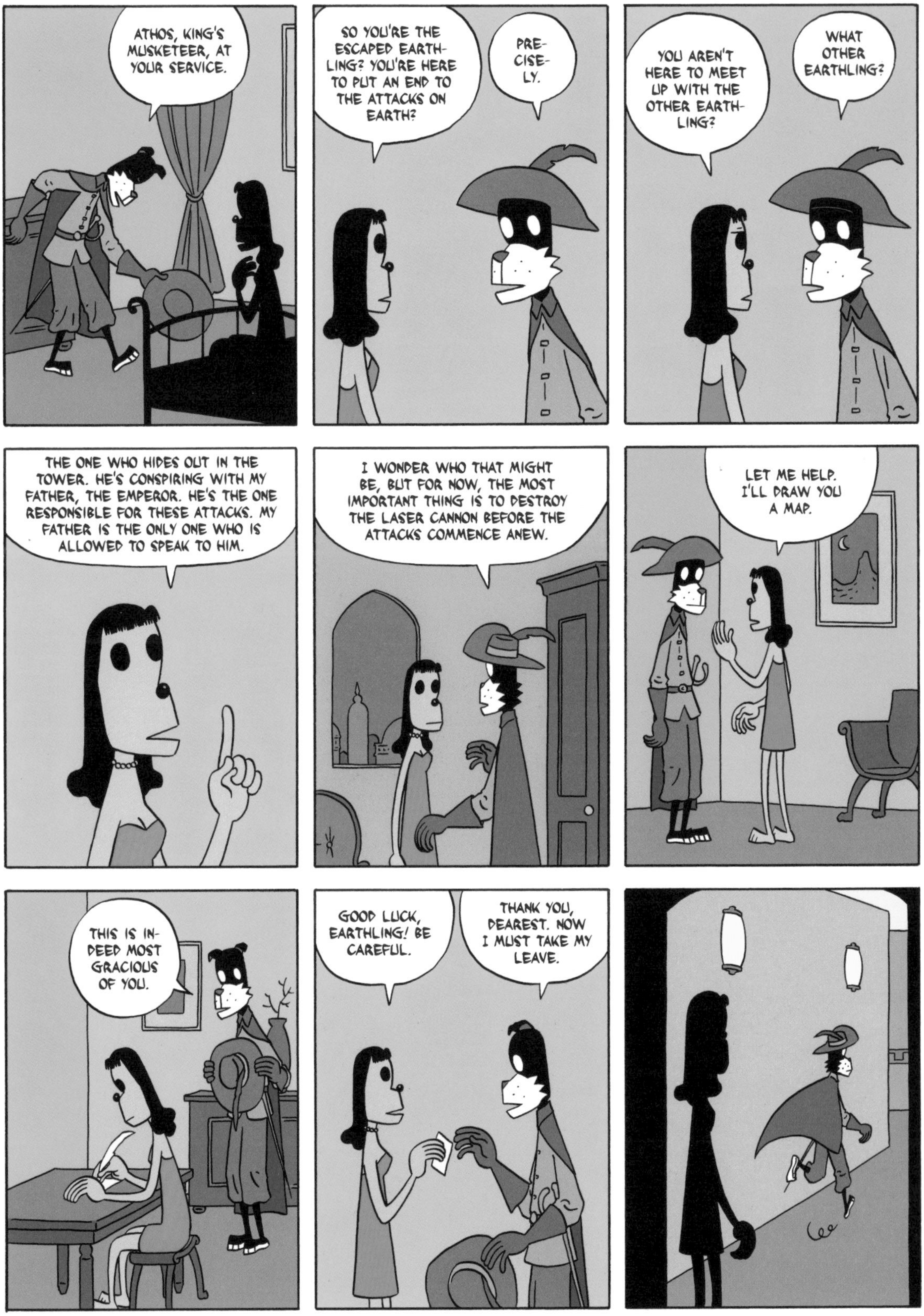
ATHOS, KING'S MUSKETEER, AT YOUR SERVICE.
SO YOU'RE THE ESCAPED EARTHLING? YOU'RE HERE TO PUT AN END TO THE ATTACKS ON EARTH?
PRECISELY.
YOU AREN'T HERE TO MEET UP WITH THE OTHER EARTHLING?
WHAT OTHER EARTHLING?
THE ONE WHO HIDES OUT IN THE TOWER. HE'S CONSPIRING WITH MY FATHER, THE EMPEROR. HE'S THE ONE RESPONSIBLE FOR THESE ATTACKS. MY FATHER IS THE ONLY ONE WHO IS ALLOWED TO SPEAK TO HIM.
I WONDER WHO THAT MIGHT BE, BUT FOR NOW, THE MOST IMPORTANT THING IS TO DESTROY THE LASER CANNON BEFORE THE ATTACKS COMMENCE ANEW.
LET ME HELP. I'LL DRAW YOU A MAP.
THIS IS INDEED MOST GRACIOUS OF YOU.
GOOD LUCK, EARTHLING! BE CAREFUL.
THANK YOU, DEAREST. NOW I MUST TAKE MY LEAVE.

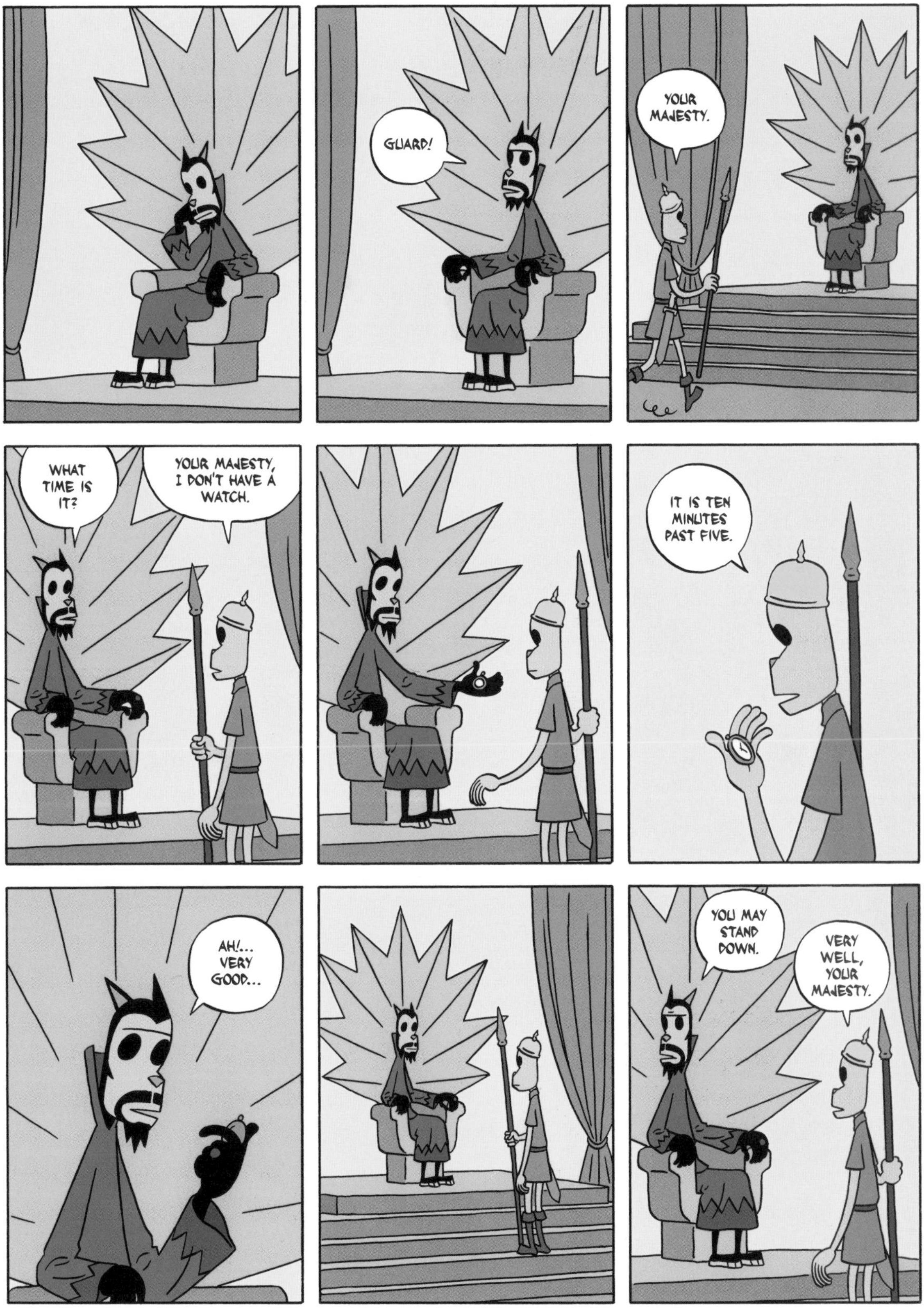
GUARD!
YOUR MAJESTY.
WHAT TIME IS IT?
YOUR MAJESTY, I DON'T HAVE A WATCH.
IT IS TEN MINUTES PAST FIVE.
AH!... VERY GOOD...
YOU MAY STAND DOWN.
VERY WELL, YOUR MAJESTY.

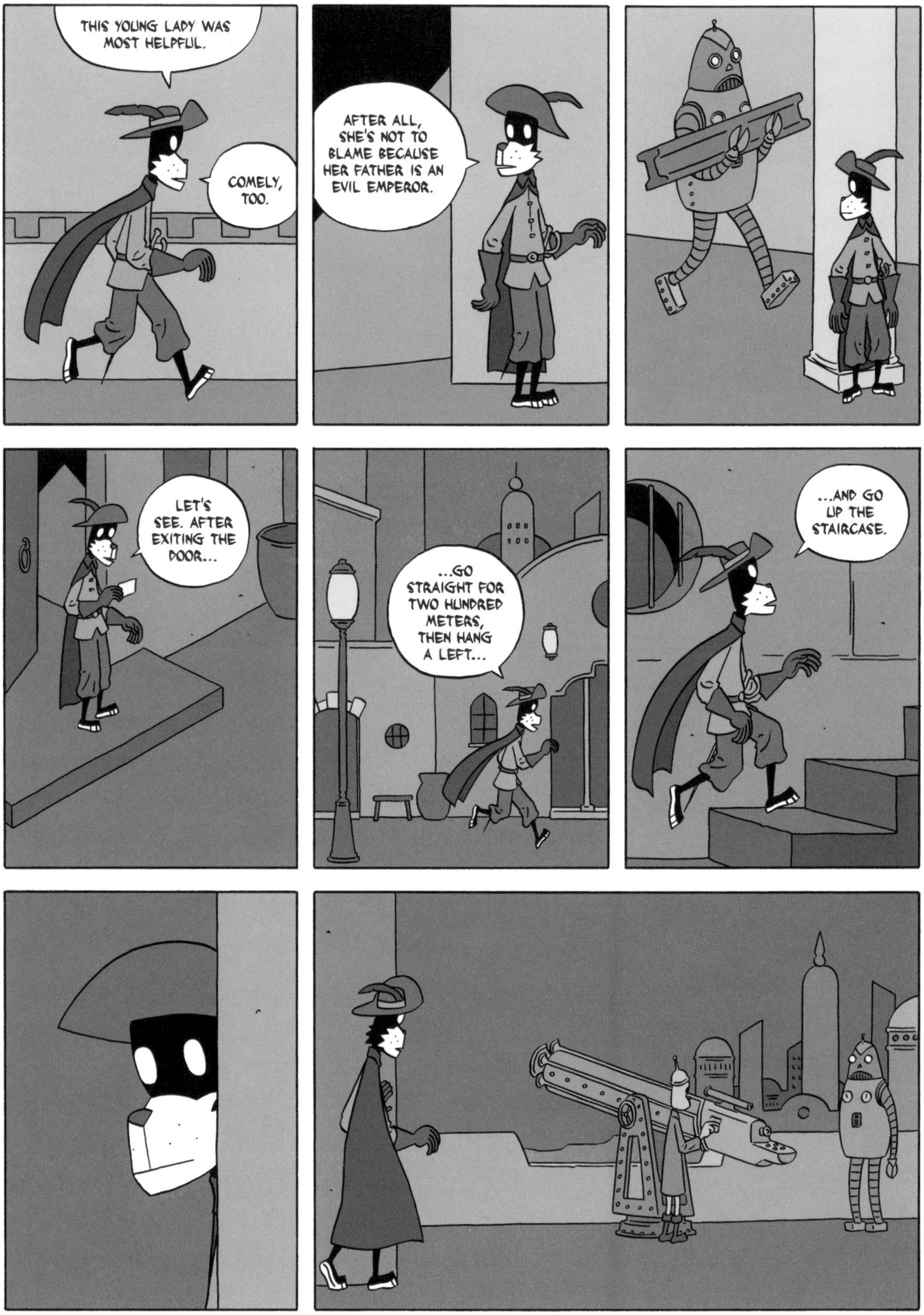
THIS YOUNG LADY WAS MOST HELPFUL.
COMELY, TOO.
AFTER ALL, SHE'S NOT TO BLAME BECAUSE HER FATHER IS AN EVIL EMPEROR.
LET'S SEE. AFTER EXITING THE DOOR...
...GO STRAIGHT FOR TWO HUNDRED METERS, THEN HANG A LEFT...
...AND GO UP THE STAIRCASE.

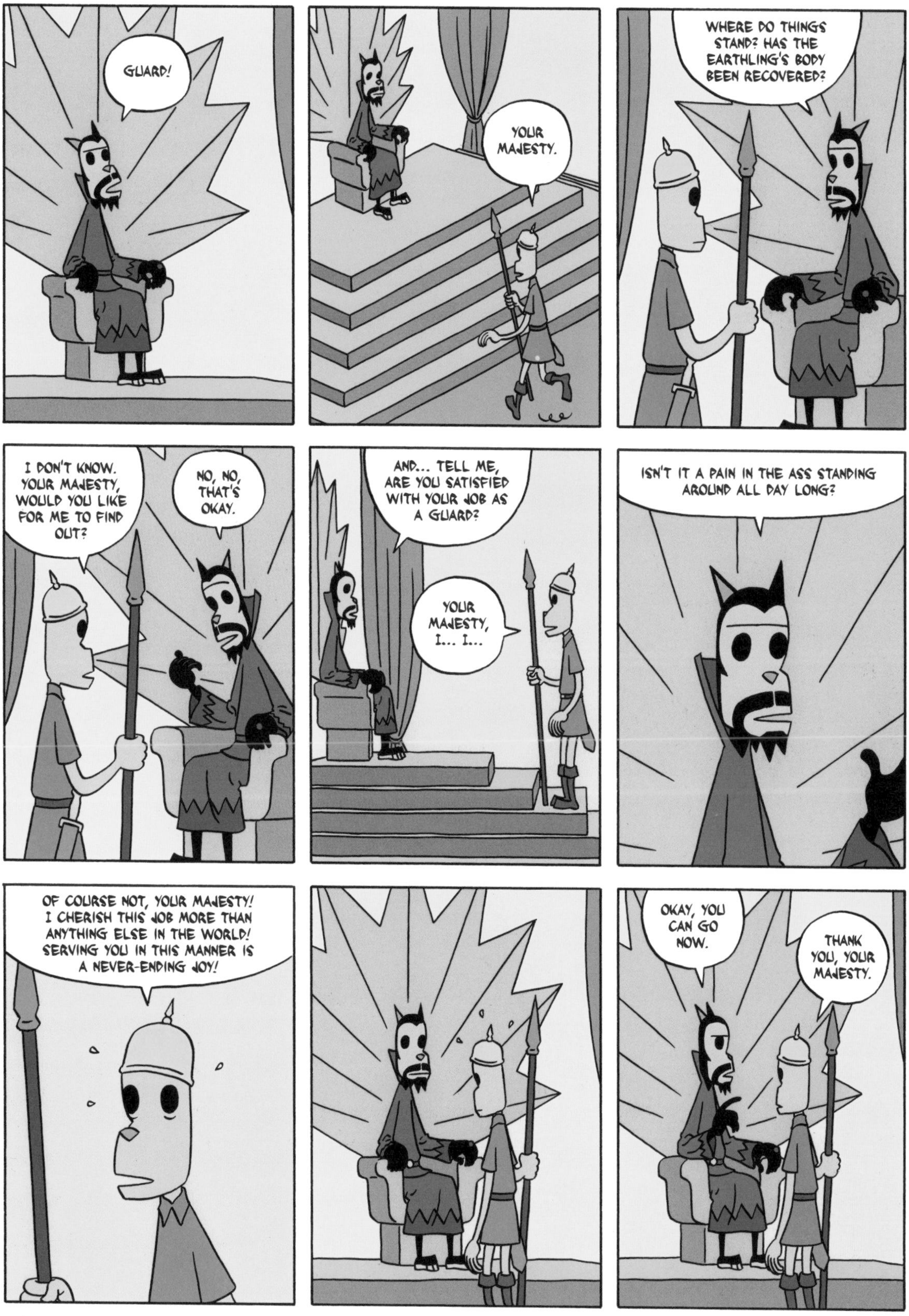
GUARD!
YOUR MAJESTY.
WHERE DO THINGS STAND? HAS THE EARTHLING'S BODY BEEN RECOVERED?
I DON'T KNOW. YOUR MAJESTY, WOULD YOU LIKE FOR ME TO FIND OUT?
NO, NO, THAT'S OKAY.
AND... TELL ME, ARE YOU SATISFIED WITH YOUR JOB AS A GUARD?
YOUR MAJESTY, I... I...
ISN'T IT A PAIN IN THE ASS STANDING AROUND ALL DAY LONG?
OF COURSE NOT, YOUR MAJESTY! I CHERISH THIS JOB MORE THAN ANYTHING ELSE IN THE WORLD! SERVING YOU IN THIS MANNER IS A NEVER-ENDING JOY!
OKAY, YOU CAN GO NOW.
THANK YOU, YOUR MAJESTY.

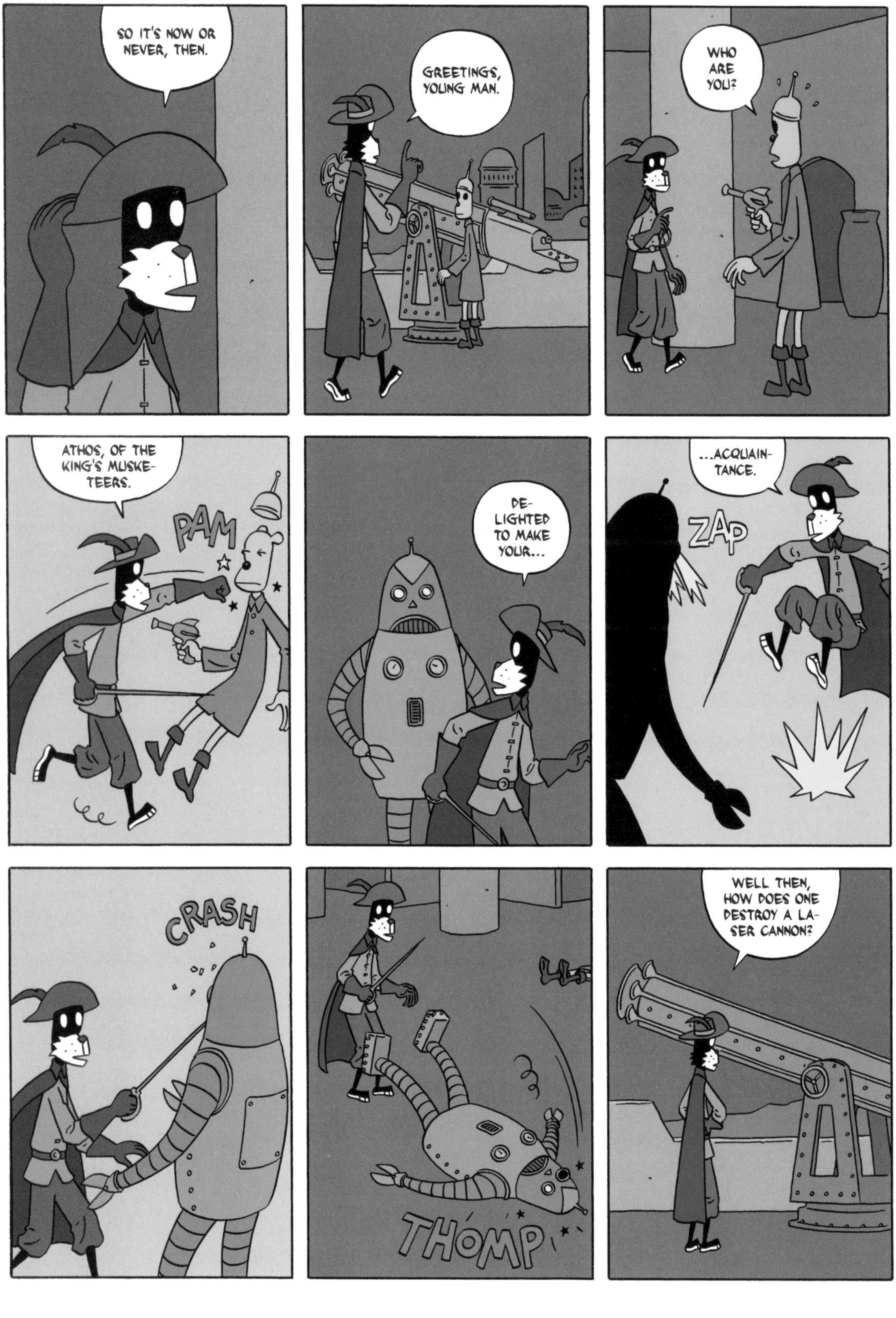
SO IT'S NOW OR NEVER, THEN.
GREETINGS, YOUNG MAN.
WHO ARE YOU?
ATHOS, OF THE KING'S MUSKE-TEERS.
PAM
DE-LIGHTED TO MAKE YOUR...
...ACQUAIN-TANCE.
ZAP
CRASH
THOMP
WELL THEN, HOW DOES ONE DESTROY A LA-SER CANNON?

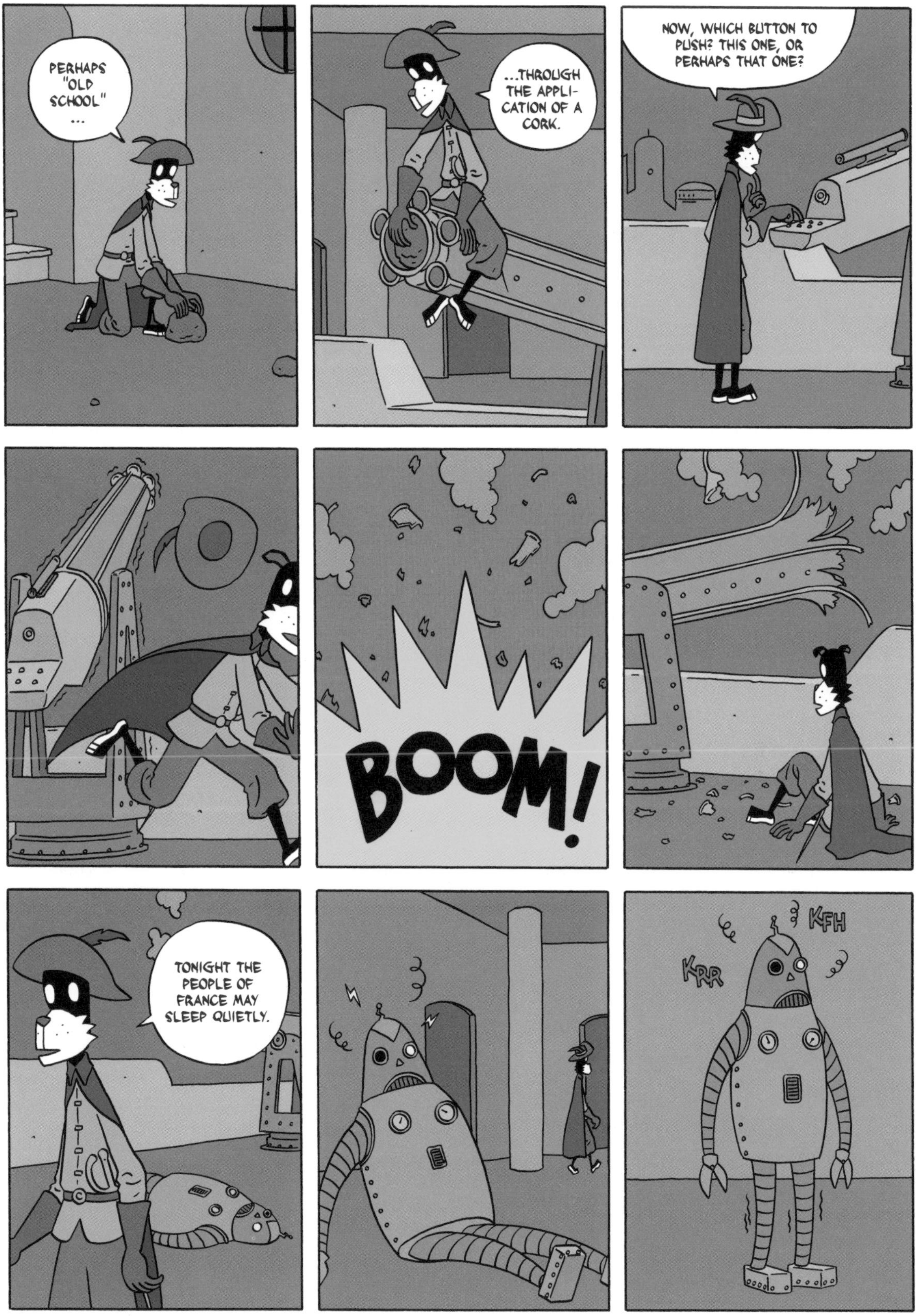
PERHAPS "OLD SCHOOL" ...
...THROUGH THE APPLI-CATION OF A CORK.
NOW, WHICH BUTTON TO PUSH? THIS ONE, OR PERHAPS THAT ONE?
BOOM!
TONIGHT THE PEOPLE OF FRANCE MAY SLEEP QUIETLY.
KPR
KFH

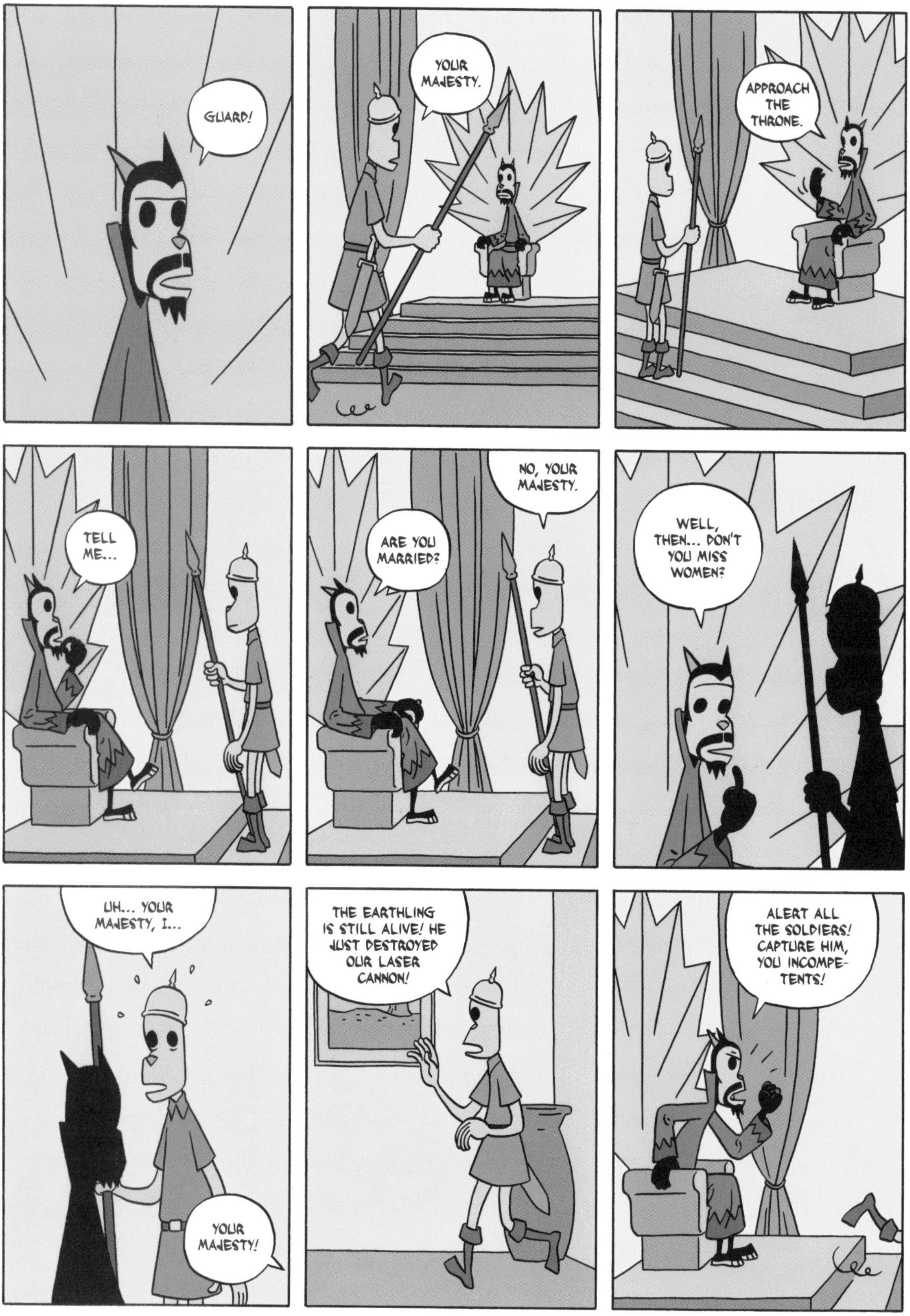
GUARD!
YOUR MAJESTY.
APPROACH THE THRONE.
TELL ME...
ARE YOU MARRIED?
NO, YOUR MAJESTY.
WELL, THEN... DON'T YOU MISS WOMEN?
UH... YOUR MAJESTY, I...
YOUR MAJESTY!
THE EARTHLING IS STILL ALIVE! HE JUST DESTROYED OUR LASER CANNON!
ALERT ALL THE SOLDIERS! CAPTURE HIM, YOU INCOMPE-TENTS!

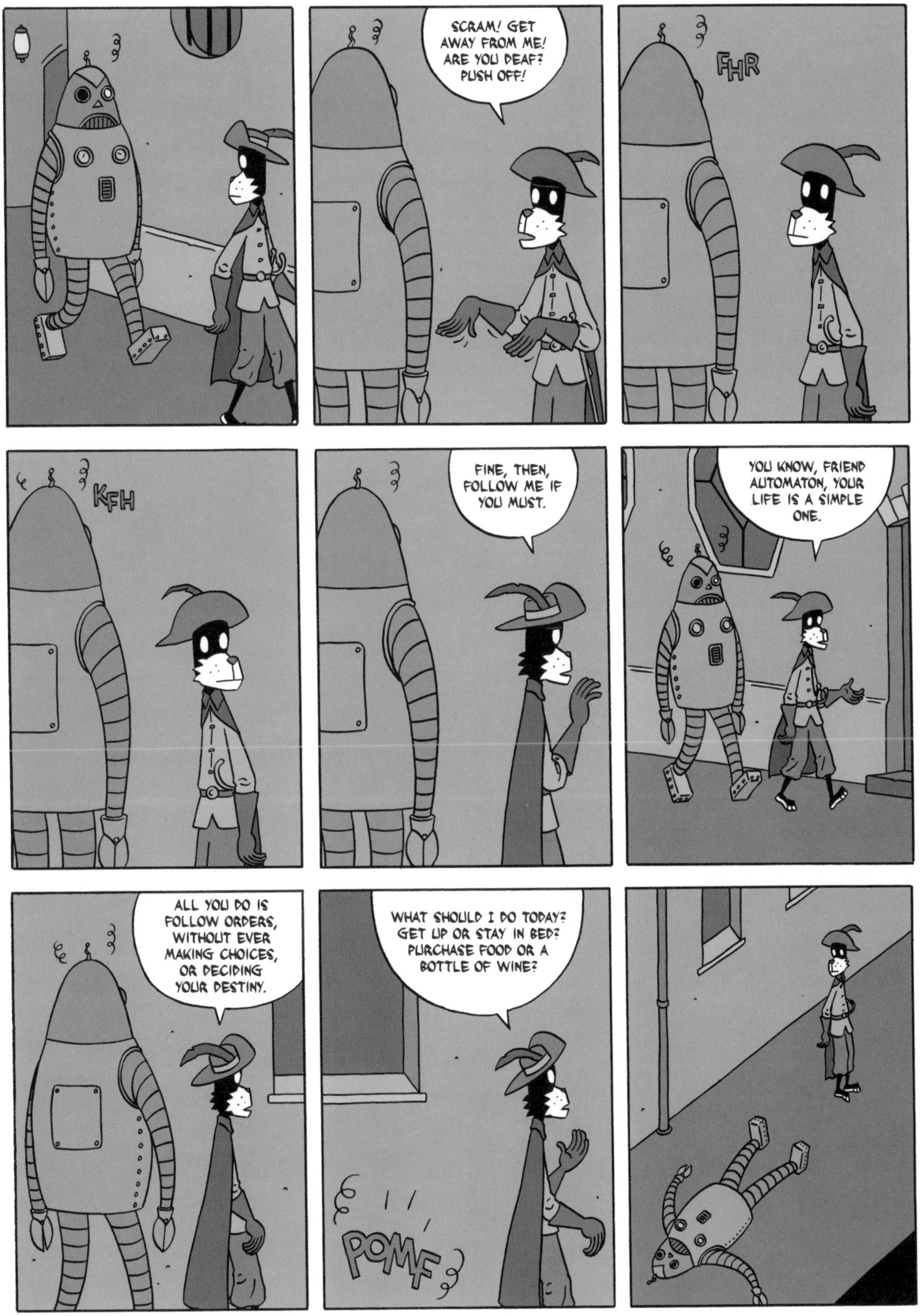
SCRAM! GET AWAY FROM ME! ARE YOU DEAF? PUSH OFF!
FHR
KFH
FINE, THEN, FOLLOW ME IF YOU MUST.
YOU KNOW, FRIEND AUTOMATON, YOUR LIFE IS A SIMPLE ONE.
ALL YOU DO IS FOLLOW ORDERS, WITHOUT EVER MAKING CHOICES, OR DECIDING YOUR DESTINY.
WHAT SHOULD I DO TODAY? GET UP OR STAY IN BED? PURCHASE FOOD OR A BOTTLE OF WINE?
POMF

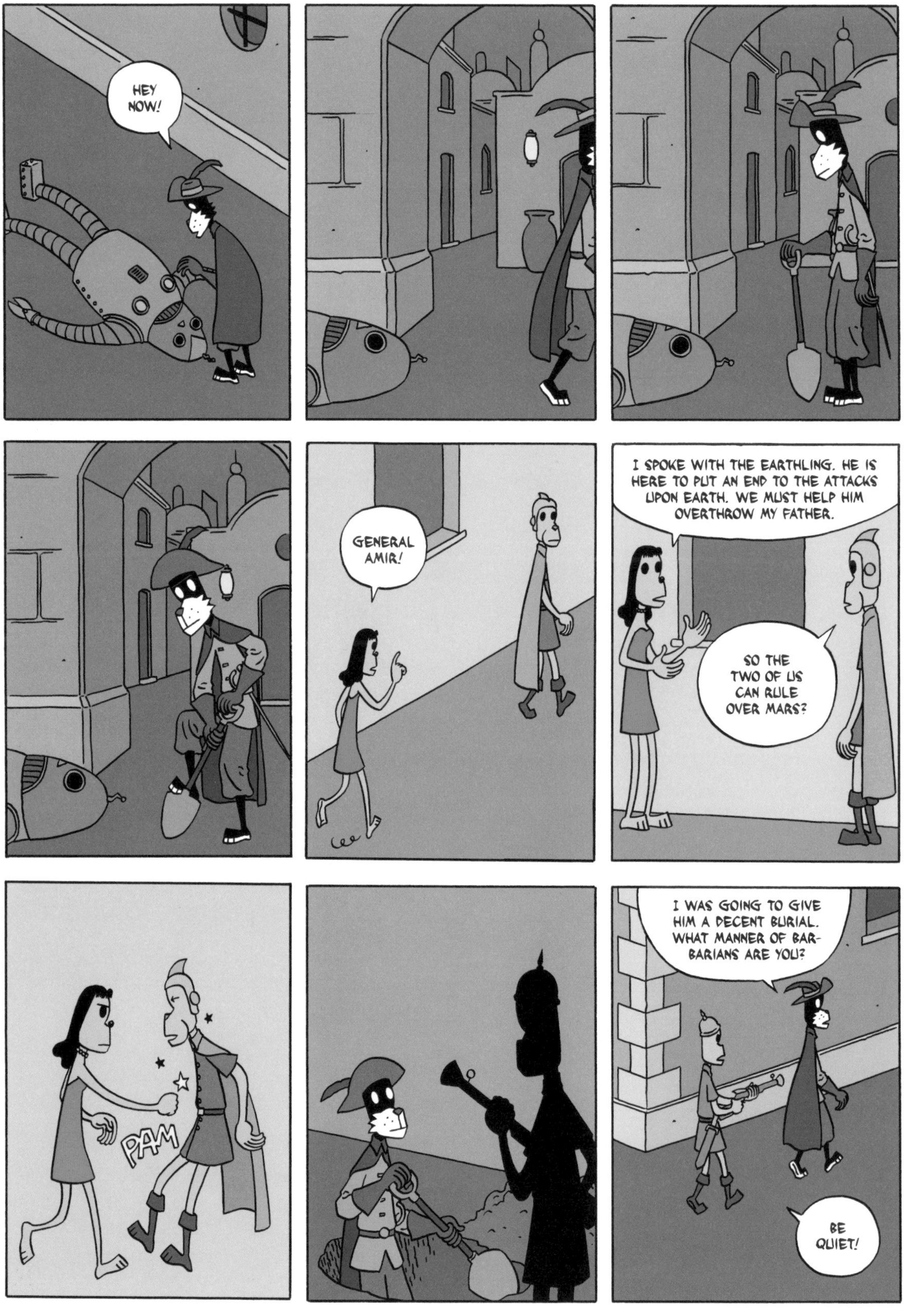

HEY NOW!
GENERAL AMIR!
I SPOKE WITH THE EARTHLING. HE IS HERE TO PUT AN END TO THE ATTACKS UPON EARTH. WE MUST HELP HIM OVERTHROW MY FATHER.
SO THE TWO OF US CAN RULE OVER MARS?
PAM
I WAS GOING TO GIVE HIM A DECENT BURIAL. WHAT MANNER OF BAR-BARIANS ARE YOU?
BE QUIET!

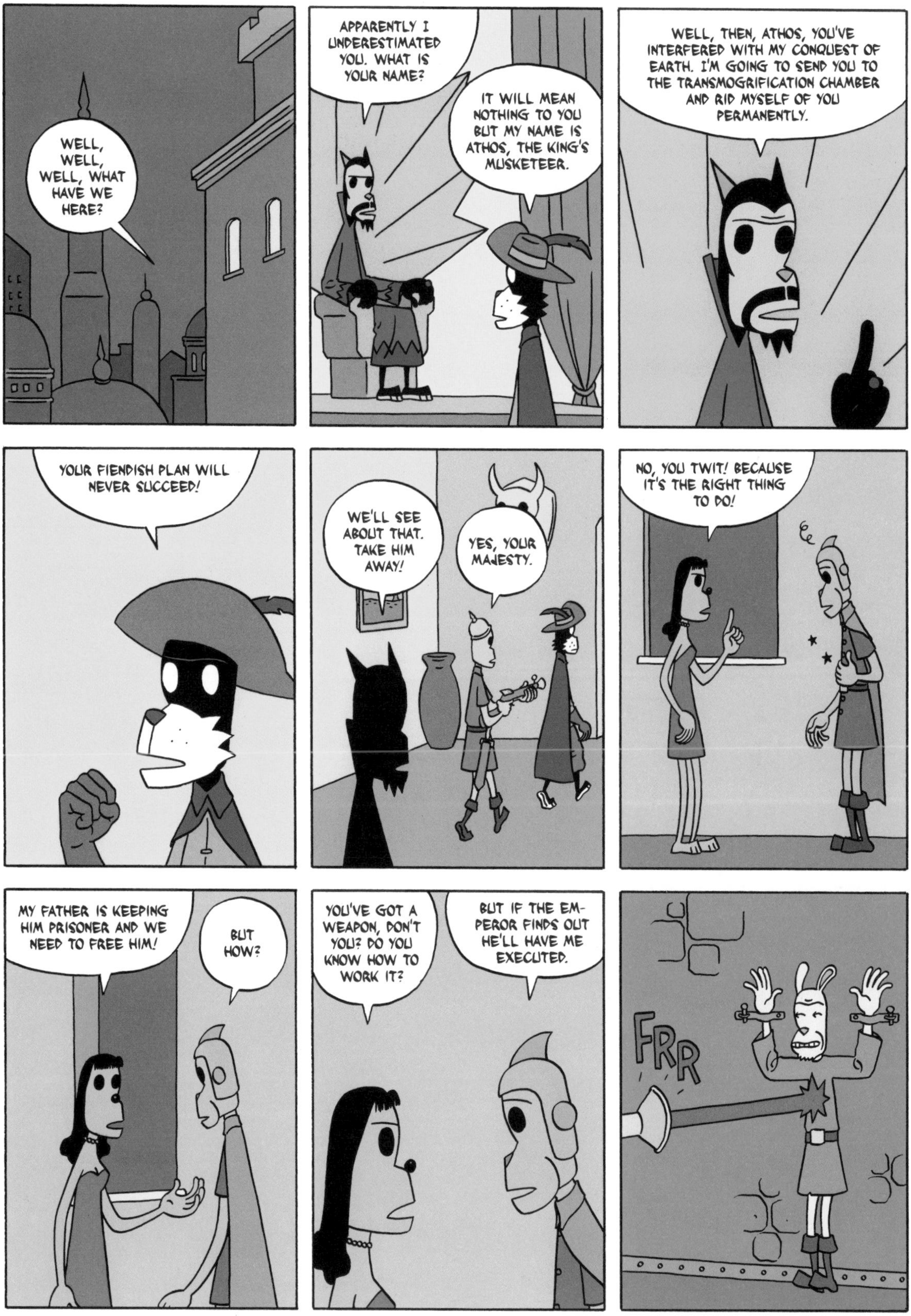
WELL, WELL, WELL, WHAT HAVE WE HERE?
APPARENTLY I UNDERESTIMATED YOU. WHAT IS YOUR NAME?
IT WILL MEAN NOTHING TO YOU BUT MY NAME IS ATHOS, THE KING'S MUSKETEER.
WELL, THEN, ATHOS, YOU'VE INTERFERED WITH MY CONQUEST OF EARTH. I'M GOING TO SEND YOU TO THE TRANSMOGRIFICATION CHAMBER AND RID MYSELF OF YOU PERMANENTLY.
YOUR FIENDISH PLAN WILL NEVER SUCCEED!
WE'LL SEE ABOUT THAT. TAKE HIM AWAY!
YES, YOUR MAJESTY.
NO, YOU TWIT! BECAUSE IT'S THE RIGHT THING TO DO!
MY FATHER IS KEEPING HIM PRISONER AND WE NEED TO FREE HIM!
BUT HOW?
YOU'VE GOT A WEAPON, DON'T YOU? DO YOU KNOW HOW TO WORK IT?
BUT IF THE EMPEROR FINDS OUT HE'LL HAVE ME EXECUTED.
FRR

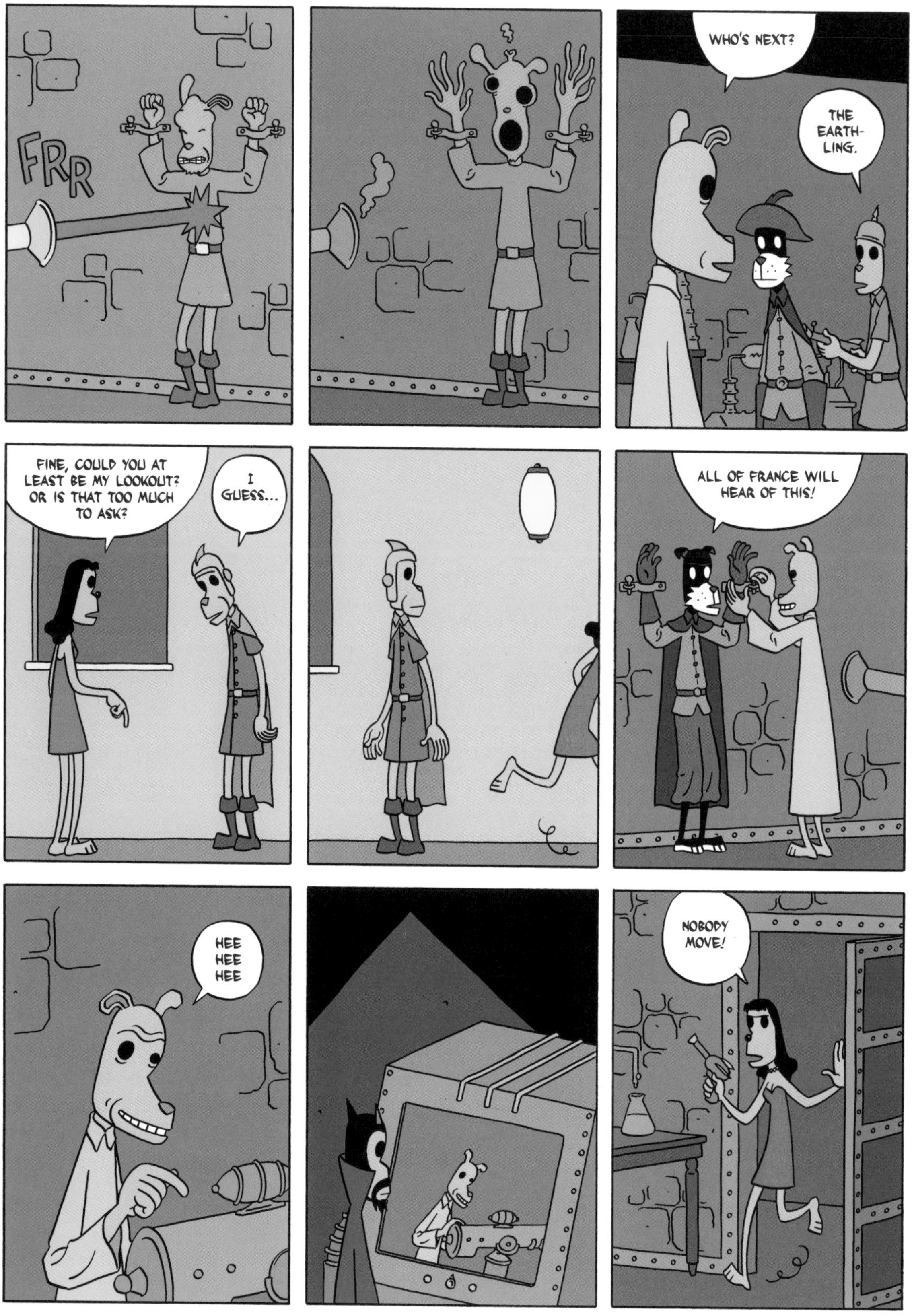
FRR
WHO'S NEXT?
THE EARTH-LING.
FINE, COULD YOU AT LEAST BE MY LOOKOUT? OR IS THAT TOO MUCH TO ASK?
I GUESS...
ALL OF FRANCE WILL HEAR OF THIS!
HEE HEE HEE
NOBODY MOVE!

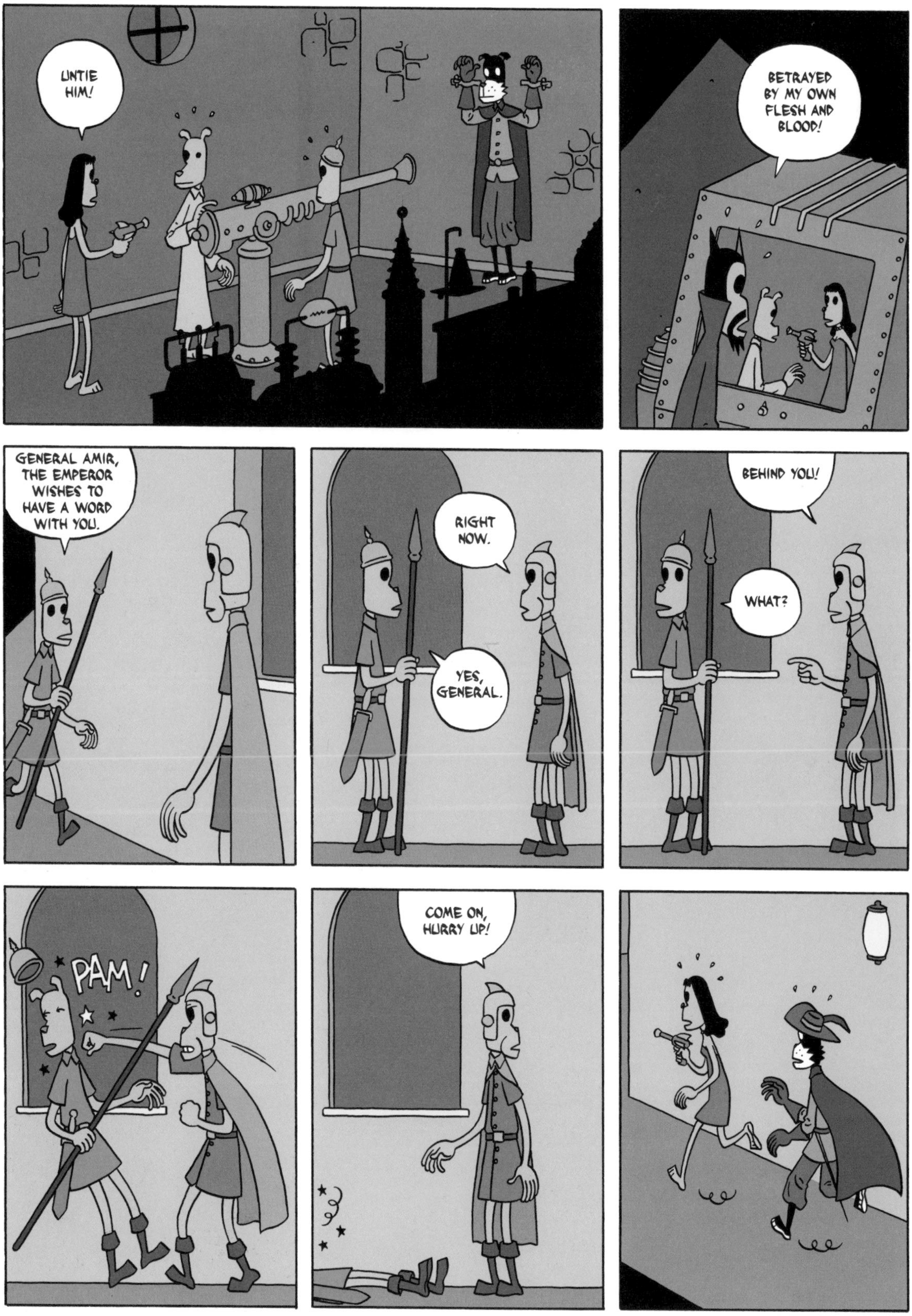
UNTIE HIM!
BETRAYED BY MY OWN FLESH AND BLOOD!
GENERAL AMIR, THE EMPEROR WISHES TO HAVE A WORD WITH YOU.
RIGHT NOW.
YES, GENERAL.
BEHIND YOU!
WHAT?
PAM!
COME ON, HURRY UP!

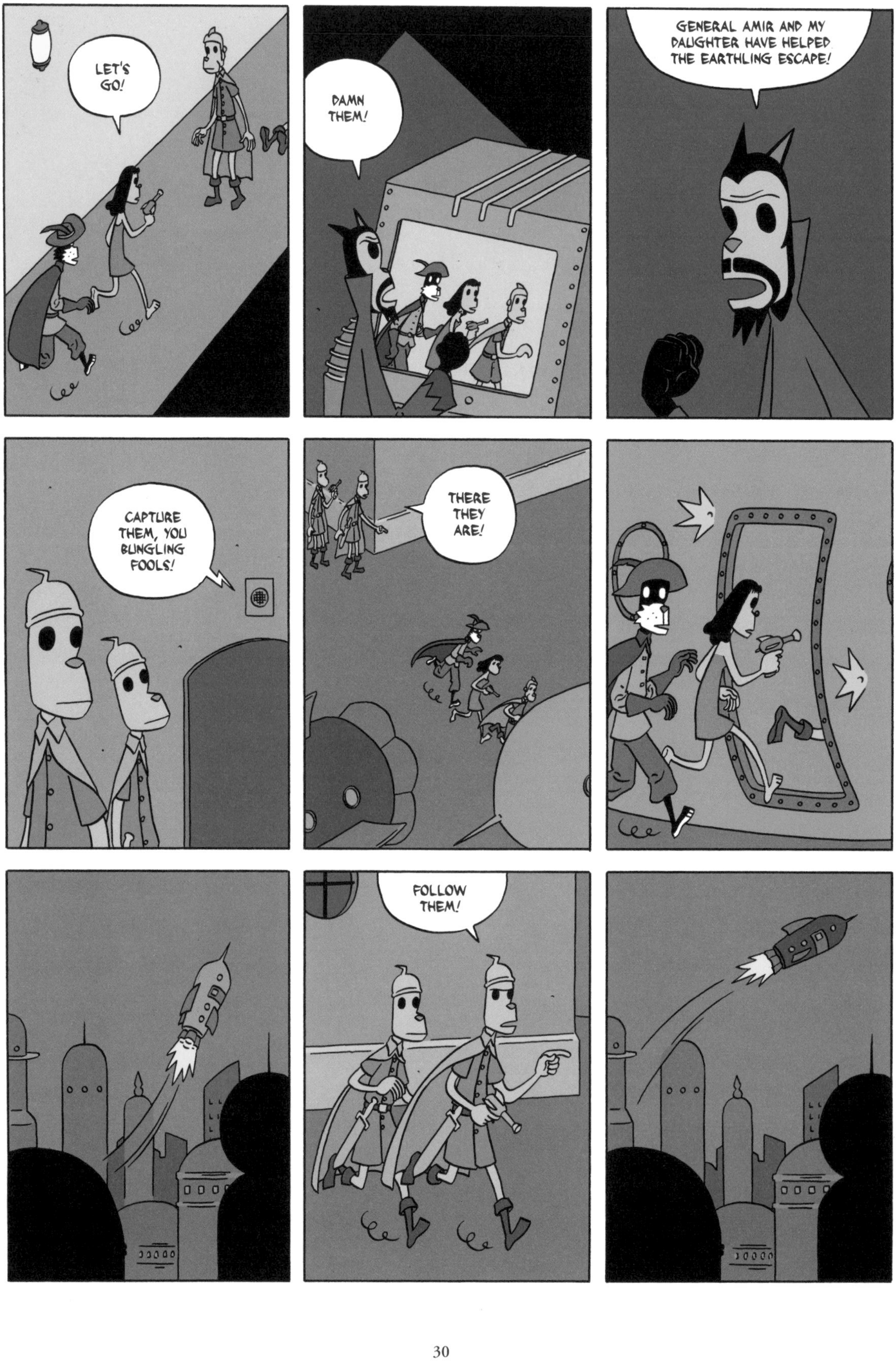
LET'S GO!
DAMN THEM!
GENERAL AMIR AND MY DAUGHTER HAVE HELPED THE EARTHLING ESCAPE!
CAPTURE THEM, YOU BUNGLING FOOLS!
THERE THEY ARE!
FOLLOW THEM!

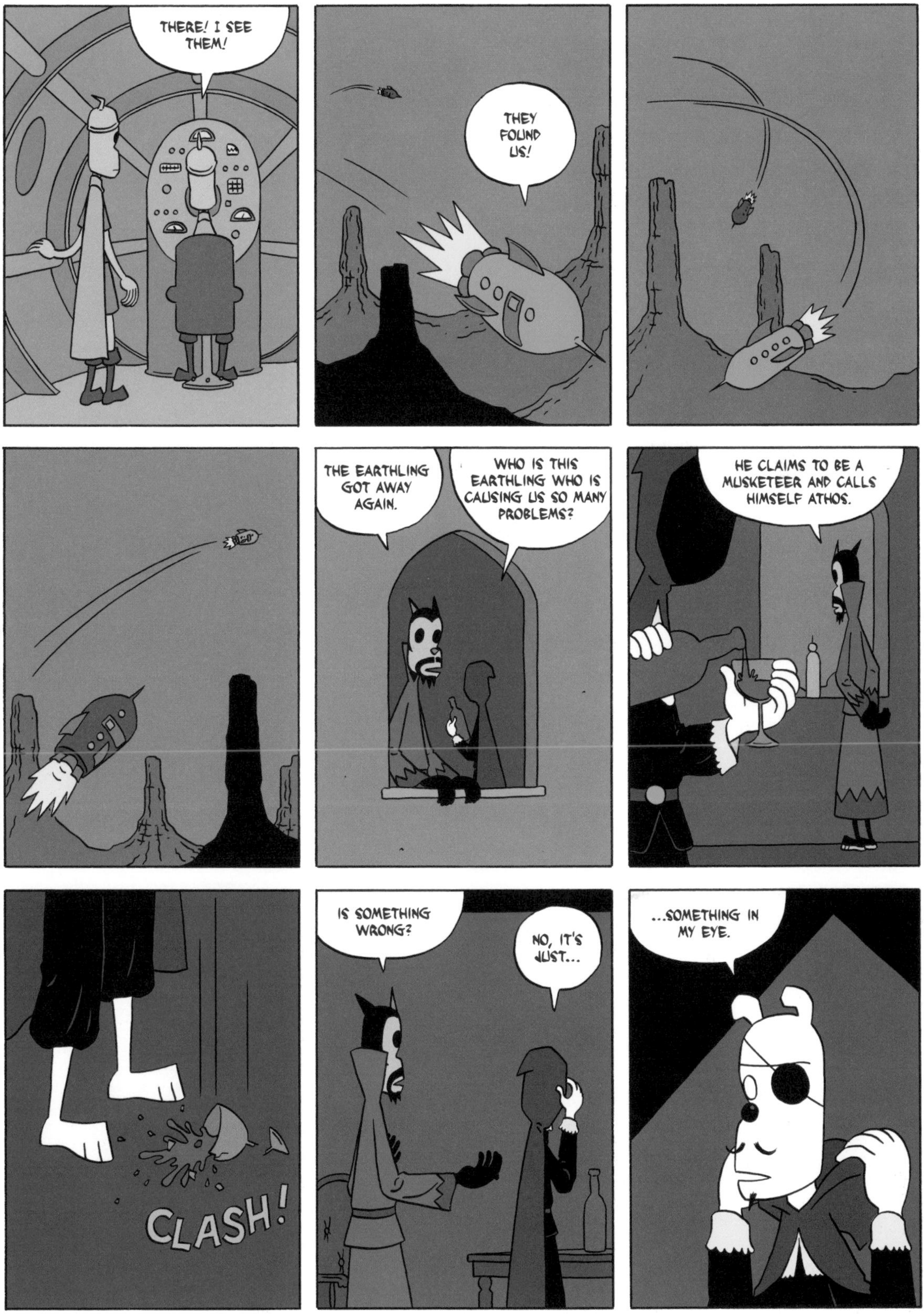
THERE! I SEE THEM!
THEY FOUND US!
THE EARTHLING GOT AWAY AGAIN.
WHO IS THIS EARTHLING WHO IS CAUSING US SO MANY PROBLEMS?
HE CLAIMS TO BE A MUSKETEER AND CALLS HIMSELF ATHOS.
CLASH!
IS SOMETHING WRONG?
NO, IT'S JUST...
...SOMETHING IN MY EYE.

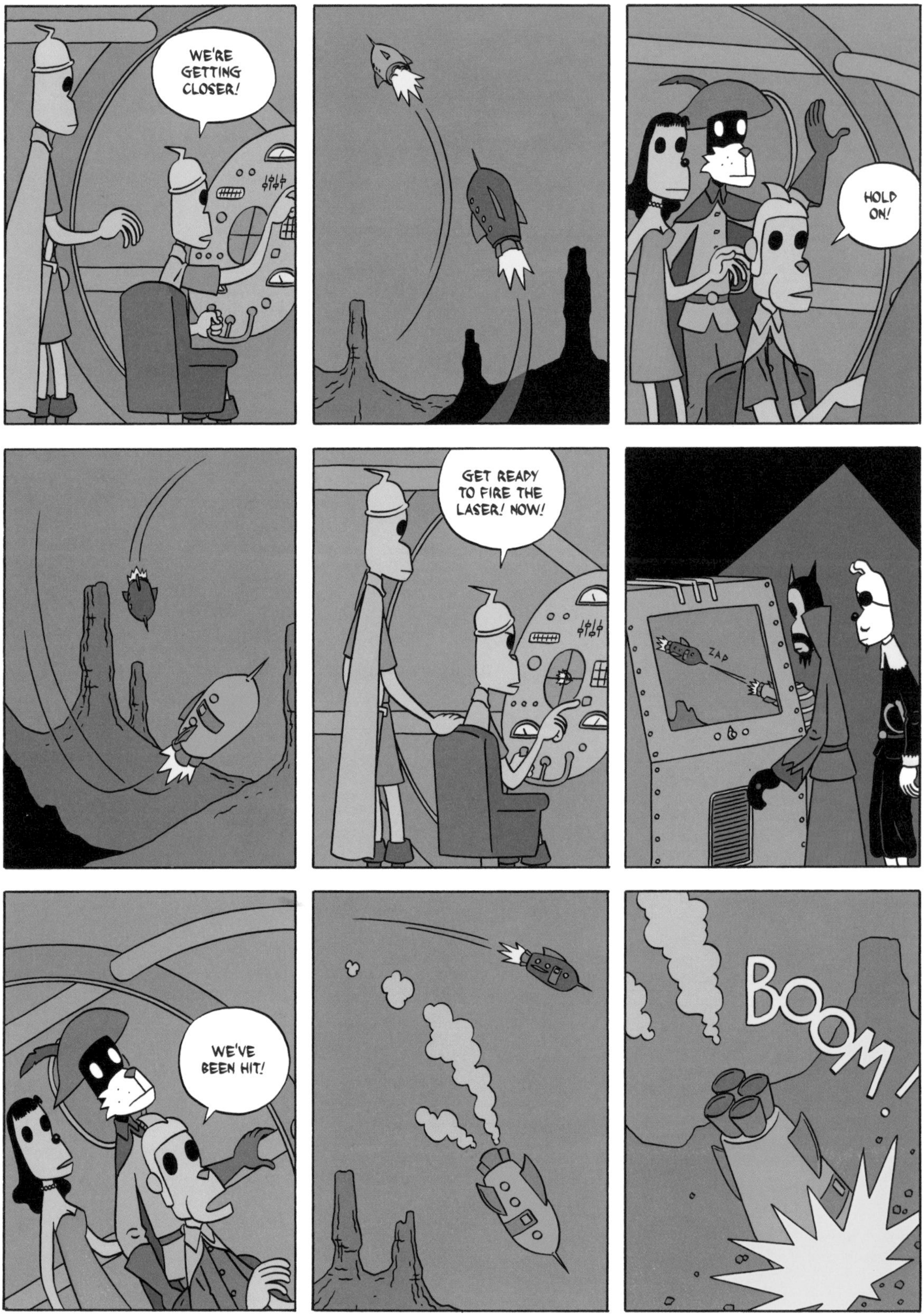
WE'RE GETTING CLOSER!
HOLD ON!
GET READY TO FIRE THE LASER! NOW!
ZAP
WE'VE BEEN HIT!
BOOM!

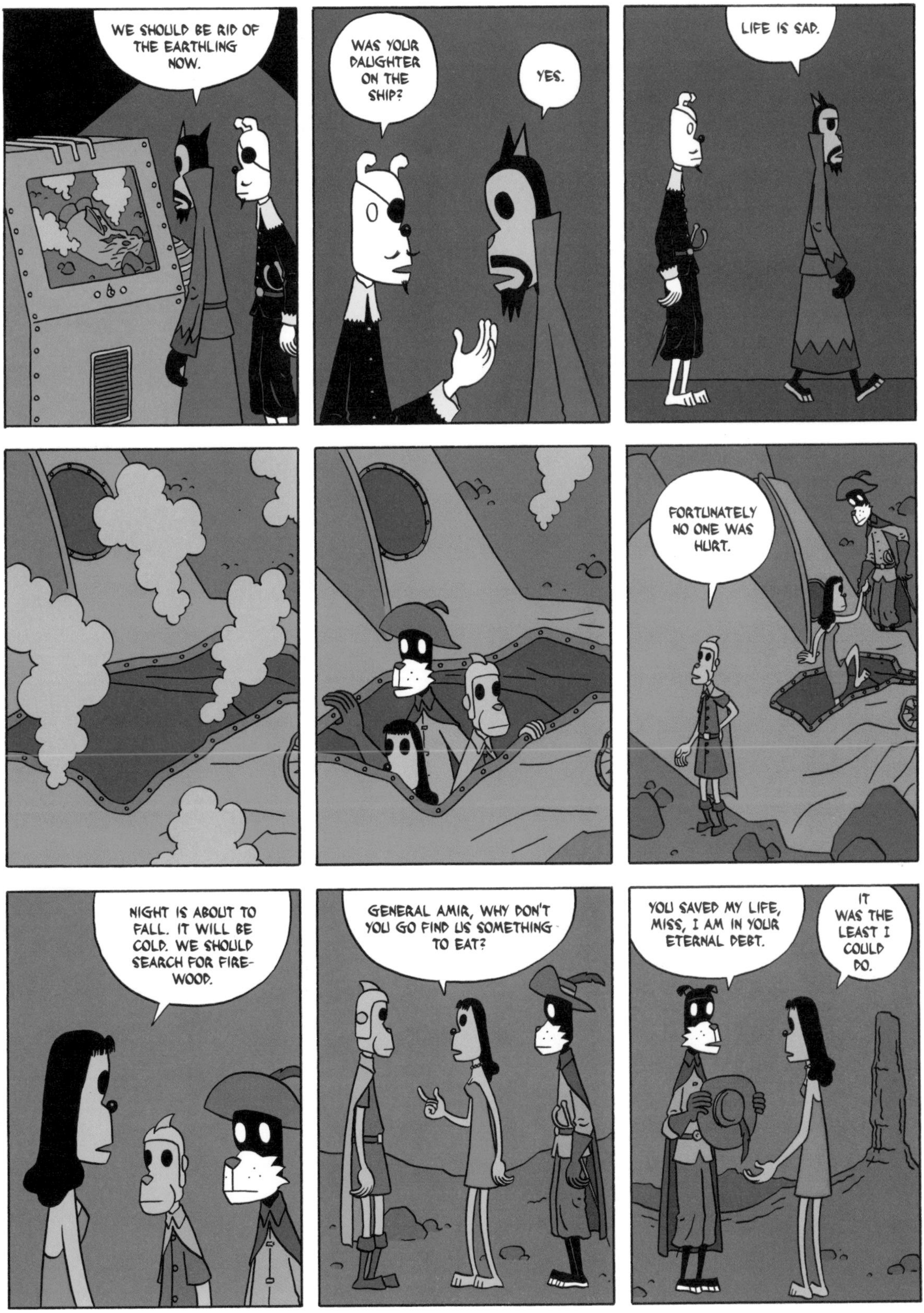
WE SHOULD BE RID OF THE EARTHLING NOW.
WAS YOUR DAUGHTER ON THE SHIP?
YES.
LIFE IS SAD.
FORTUNATELY NO ONE WAS HURT.
NIGHT IS ABOUT TO FALL. IT WILL BE COLD. WE SHOULD SEARCH FOR FIRE-WOOD.
GENERAL AMIR, WHY DON'T YOU GO FIND US SOMETHING TO EAT?
YOU SAVED MY LIFE, MISS, I AM IN YOUR ETERNAL DEBT.
IT WAS THE LEAST I COULD DO.

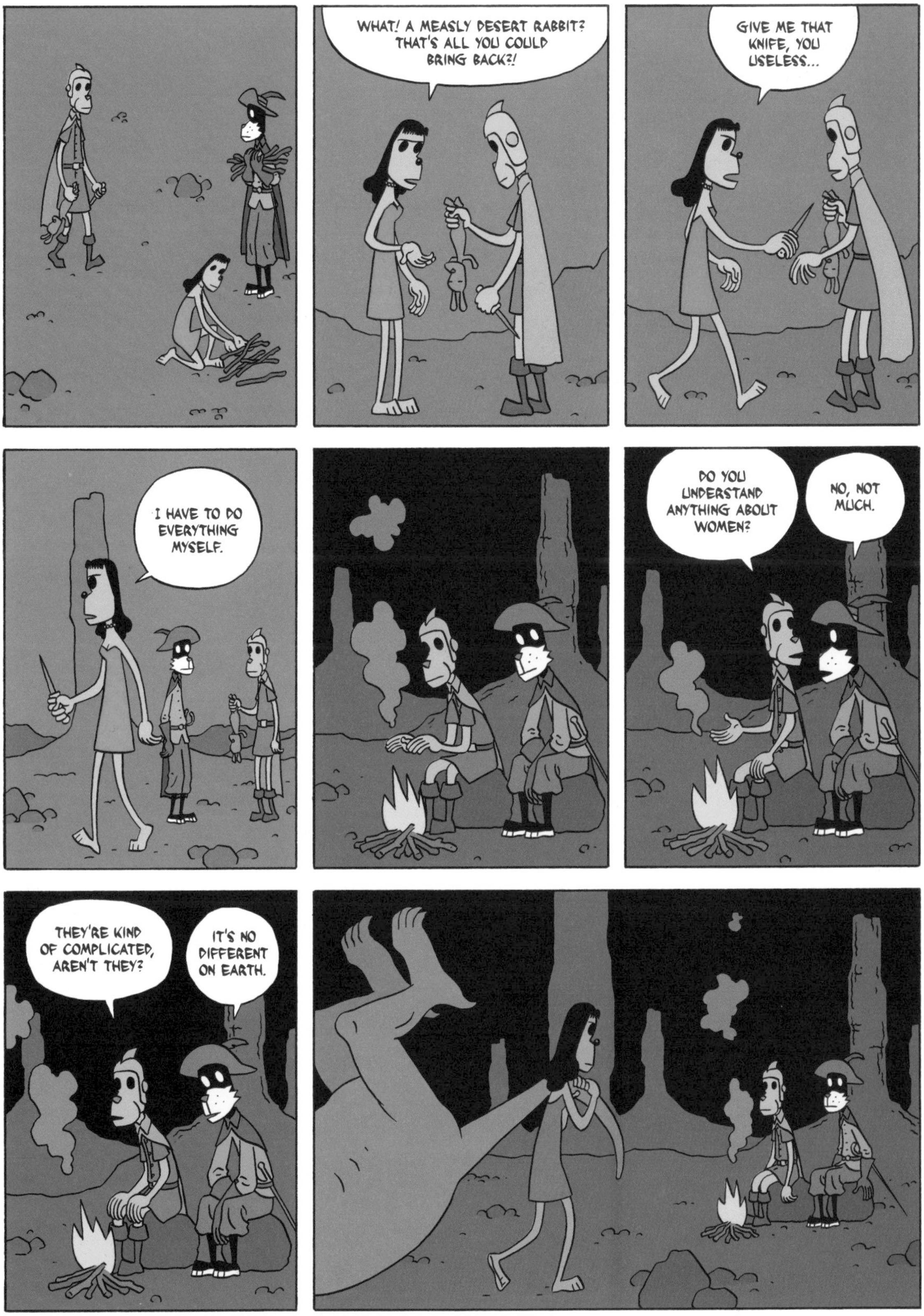
WHAT! A MEASLY DESERT RABBIT? THAT'S ALL YOU COULD BRING BACK?!
GIVE ME THAT KNIFE, YOU USELESS...
I HAVE TO DO EVERYTHING MYSELF.
DO YOU UNDERSTAND ANYTHING ABOUT WOMEN?
NO, NOT MUCH.
THEY'RE KIND OF COMPLICATED, AREN'T THEY?
IT'S NO DIFFERENT ON EARTH.

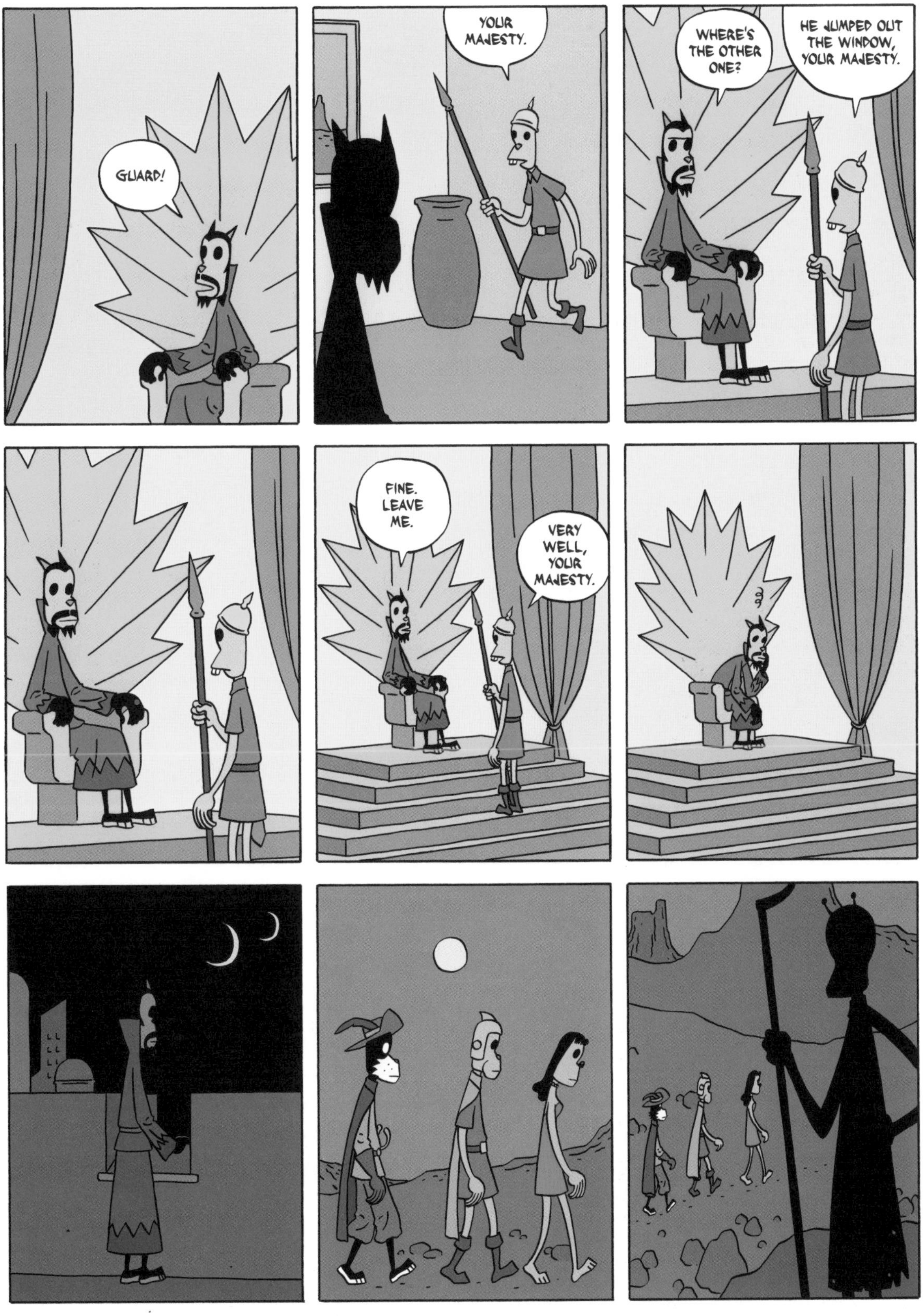
GUARD!
YOUR MAJESTY.
WHERE'S THE OTHER ONE?
HE JUMPED OUT THE WINDOW, YOUR MAJESTY.
FINE. LEAVE ME.
VERY WELL, YOUR MAJESTY.

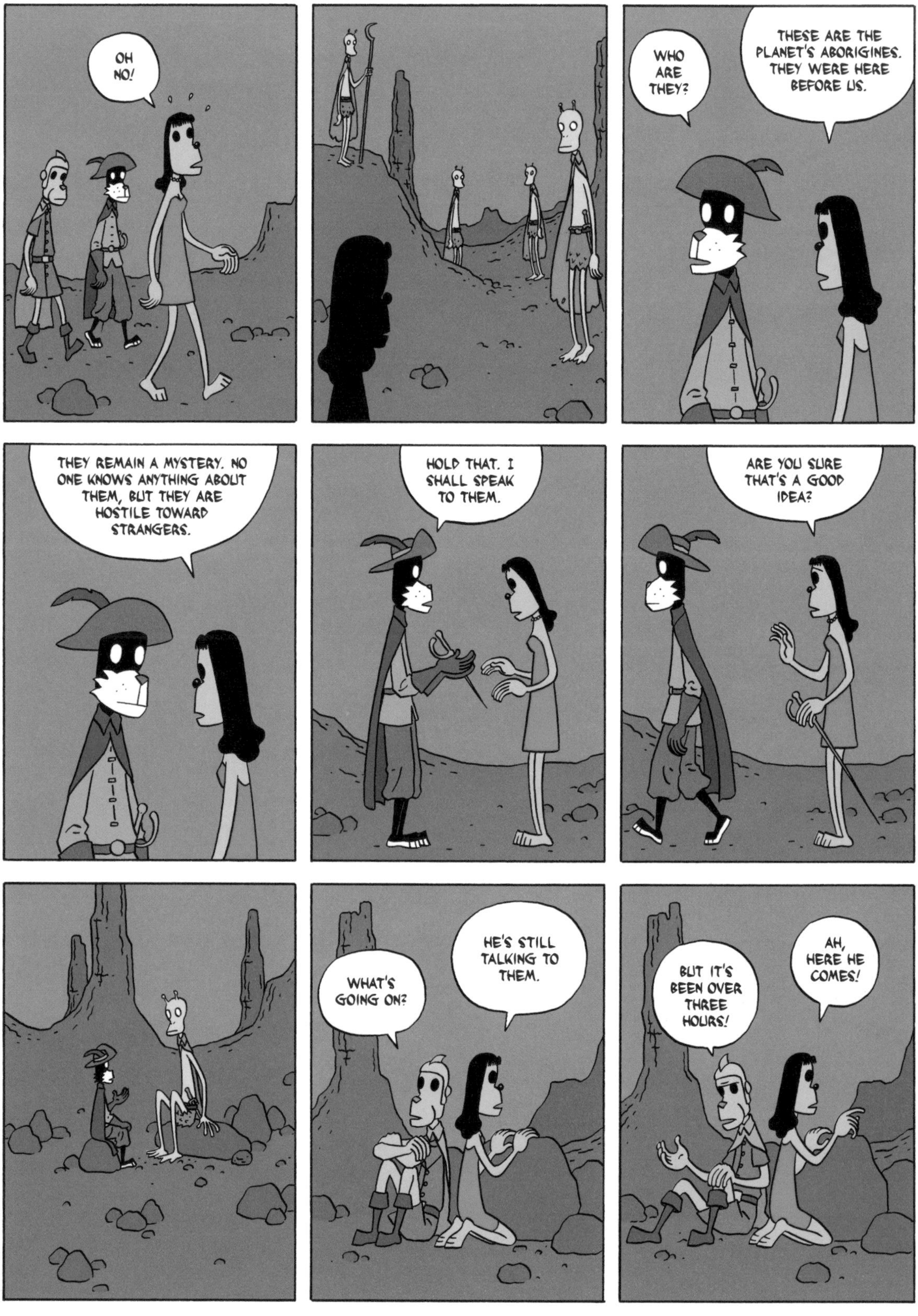
OH NO!
WHO ARE THEY?
THESE ARE THE PLANET'S ABORIGINES. THEY WERE HERE BEFORE US.
THEY REMAIN A MYSTERY. NO ONE KNOWS ANYTHING ABOUT THEM, BUT THEY ARE HOSTILE TOWARD STRANGERS.
HOLD THAT. I SHALL SPEAK TO THEM.
ARE YOU SURE THAT'S A GOOD IDEA?
WHAT'S GOING ON?
HE'S STILL TALKING TO THEM.
BUT IT'S BEEN OVER THREE HOURS!
AH, HERE HE COMES!

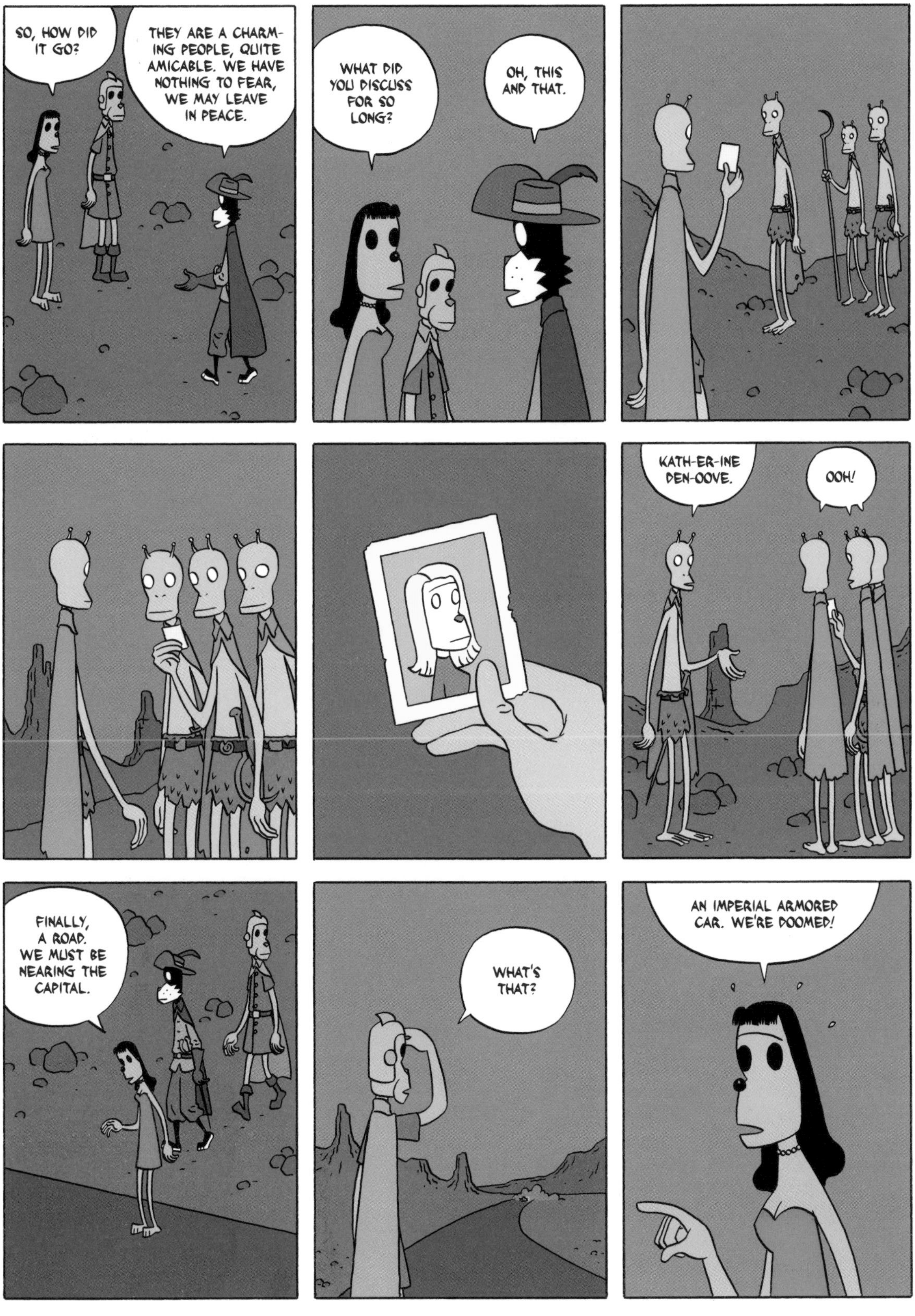
SO, HOW DID IT GO?
THEY ARE A CHARMING PEOPLE, QUITE AMICABLE. WE HAVE NOTHING TO FEAR, WE MAY LEAVE IN PEACE.
WHAT DID YOU DISCUSS FOR SO LONG?
OH, THIS AND THAT.
KATH-ER-INE DEN-OOVE.
OOH!
FINALLY, A ROAD. WE MUST BE NEARING THE CAPITAL.
WHAT'S THAT?
AN IMPERIAL ARMORED CAR. WE'RE DOOMED!

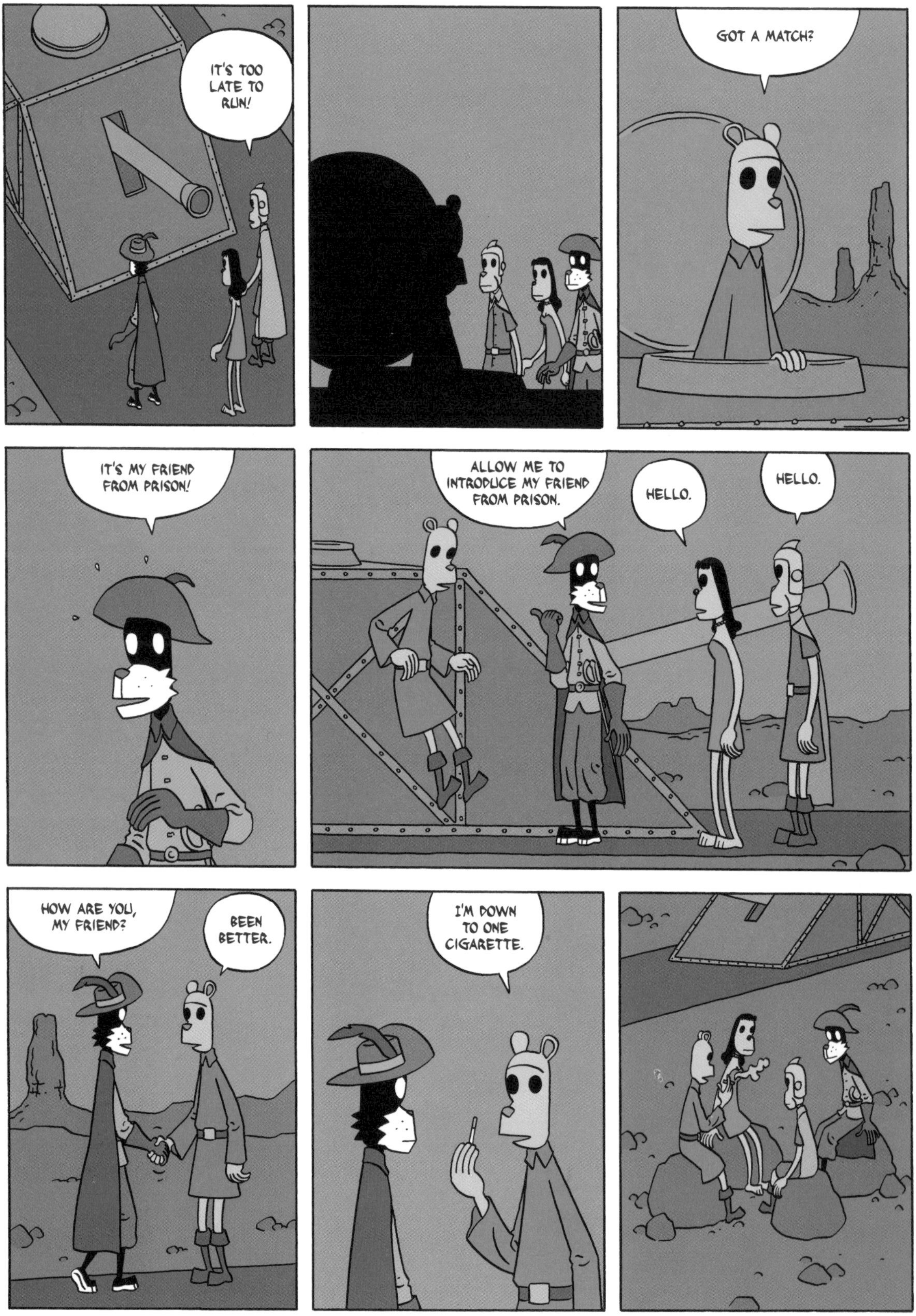
IT'S TOO LATE TO RUN!
GOT A MATCH?
IT'S MY FRIEND FROM PRISON!
ALLOW ME TO INTRODUCE MY FRIEND FROM PRISON.
HELLO.
HELLO.
HOW ARE YOU, MY FRIEND?
BEEN BETTER.
I'M DOWN TO ONE CIGARETTE.

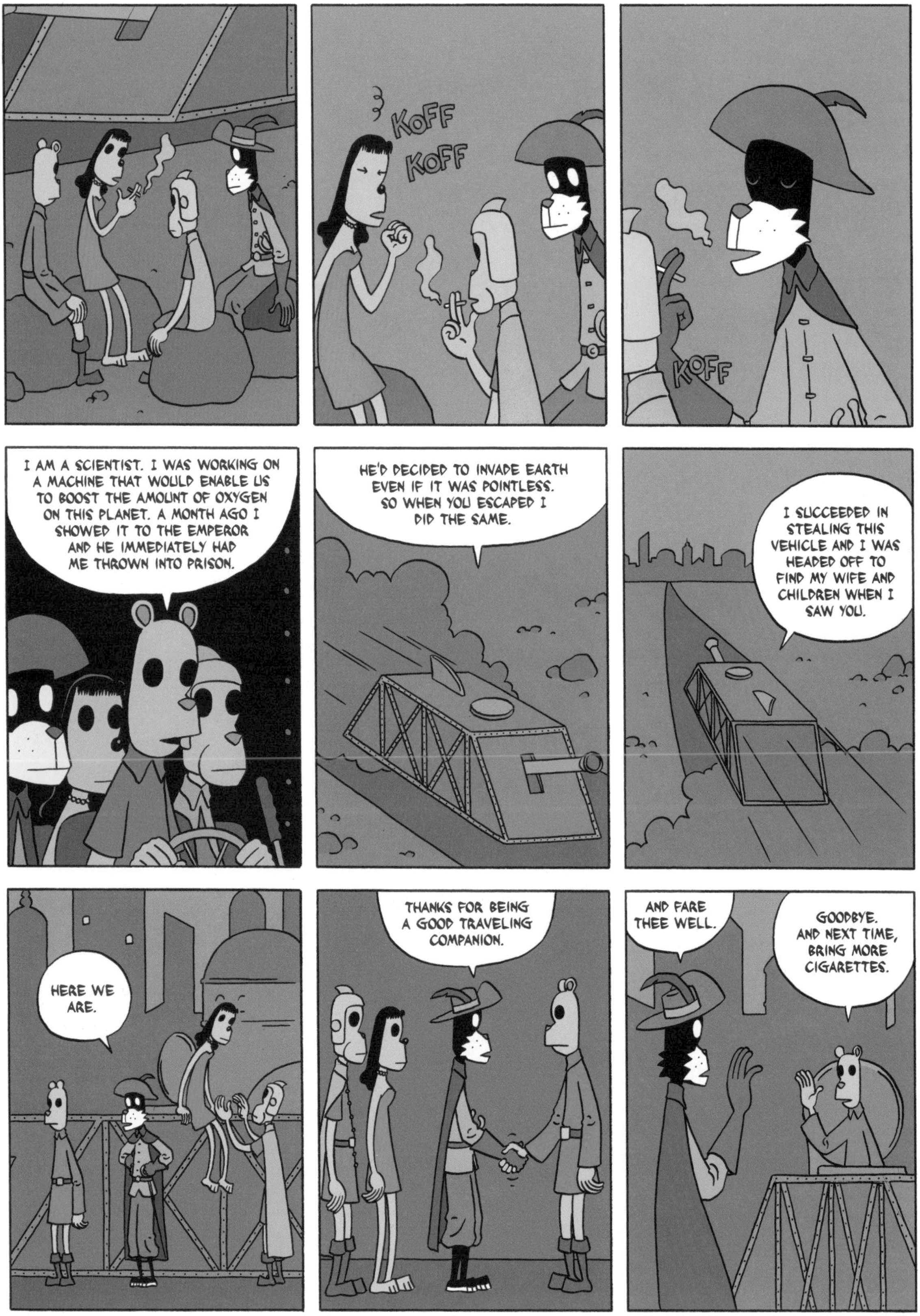
KOFF
KOFF
KOFF
I AM A SCIENTIST. I WAS WORKING ON A MACHINE THAT WOULD ENABLE US TO BOOST THE AMOUNT OF OXYGEN ON THIS PLANET. A MONTH AGO I SHOWED IT TO THE EMPEROR AND HE IMMEDIATELY HAD ME THROWN INTO PRISON.
HE'D DECIDED TO INVADE EARTH EVEN IF IT WAS POINTLESS. SO WHEN YOU ESCAPED I DID THE SAME.
I SUCCEEDED IN STEALING THIS VEHICLE AND I WAS HEADED OFF TO FIND MY WIFE AND CHILDREN WHEN I SAW YOU.
HERE WE ARE.
THANKS FOR BEING A GOOD TRAVELING COMPANION.
AND FARE THEE WELL.
GOODBYE. AND NEXT TIME, BRING MORE CIGARETTES.

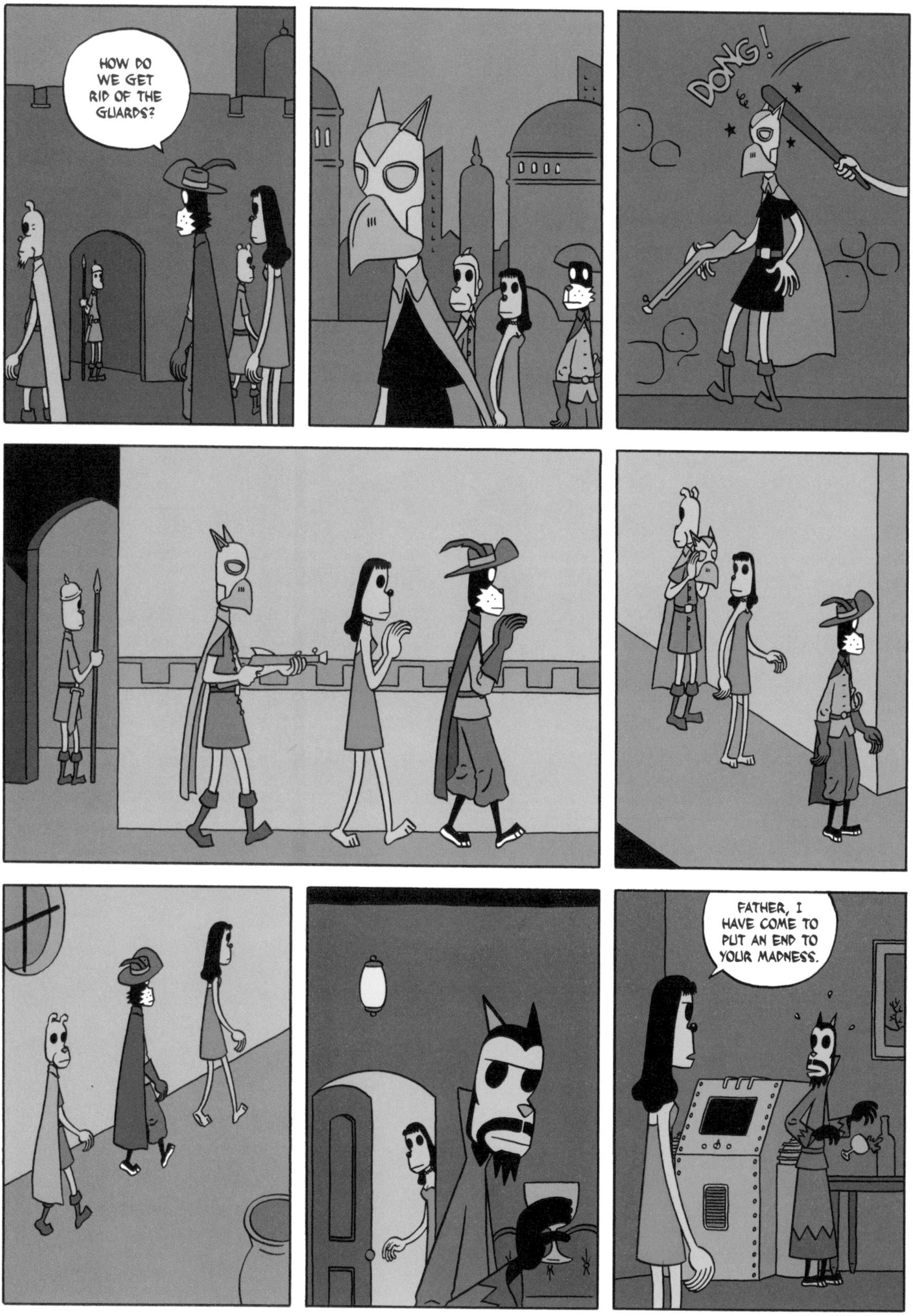
HOW DO WE GET RID OF THE GUARDS?
DONG!
FATHER, I HAVE COME TO PUT AN END TO YOUR MADNESS.

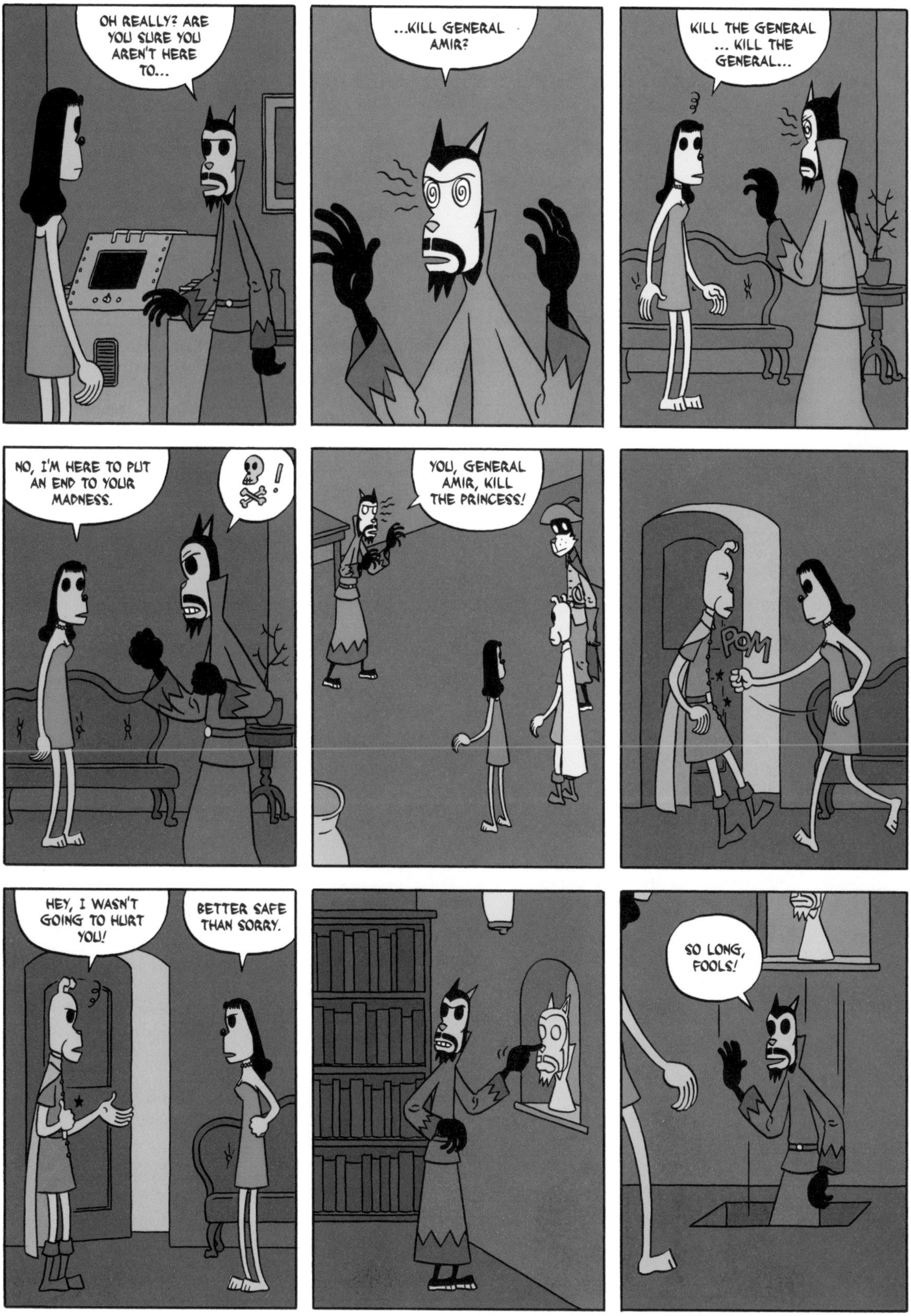
OH REALLY? ARE YOU SURE YOU AREN'T HERE TO...
...KILL GENERAL AMIR?
KILL THE GENERAL ... KILL THE GENERAL...
NO, I'M HERE TO PUT AN END TO YOUR MADNESS.
!
YOU, GENERAL AMIR, KILL THE PRINCESS!
POM
HEY, I WASN'T GOING TO HURT YOU!
BETTER SAFE THAN SORRY.
SO LONG, FOOLS!

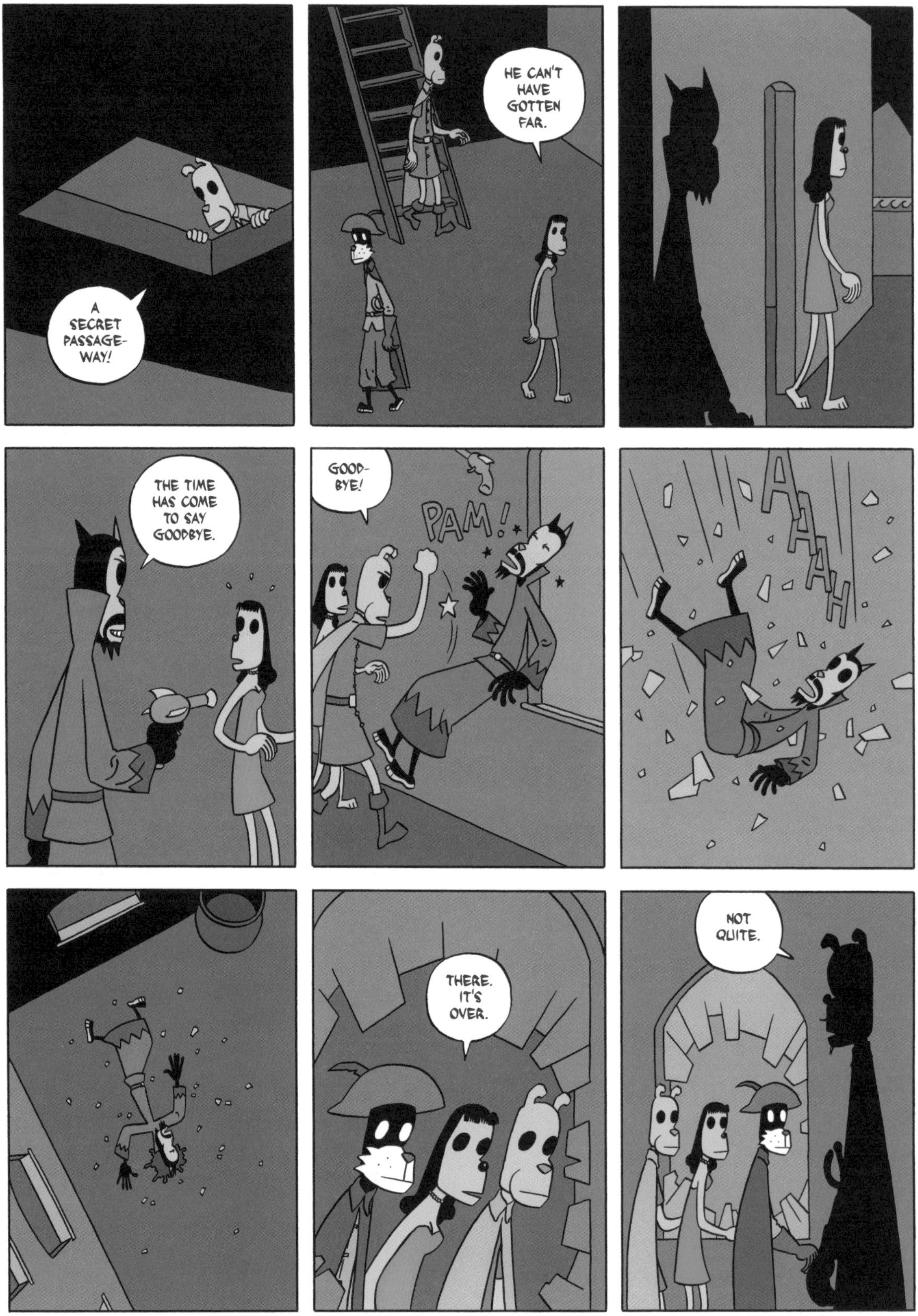
A SECRET PASSAGE-WAY!
HE CAN'T HAVE GOTTEN FAR.
THE TIME HAS COME TO SAY GOODBYE.
GOOD-BYE!
PAM!
AAAAH
THERE. IT'S OVER.
NOT QUITE.

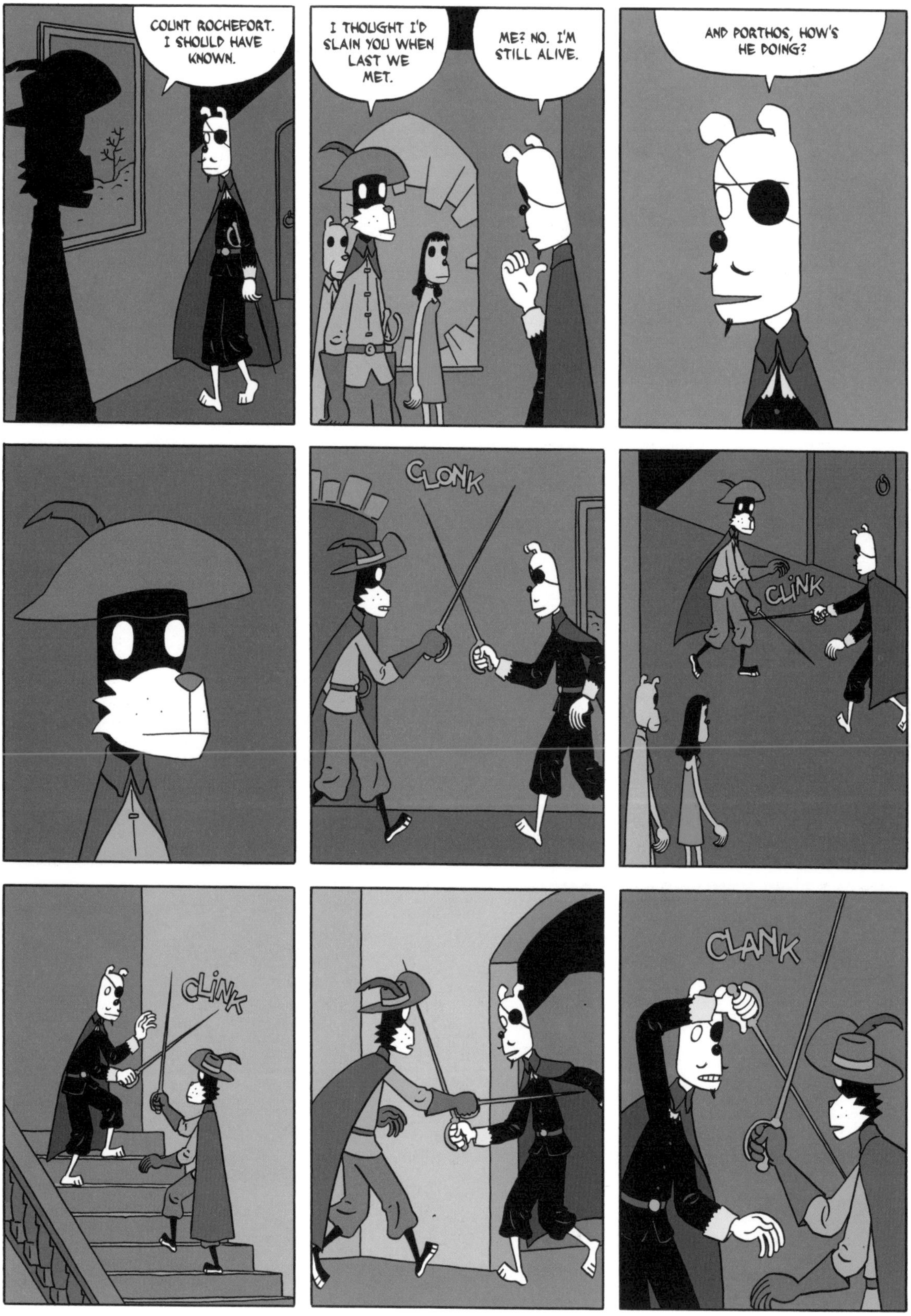
COUNT ROCHEFORT. I SHOULD HAVE KNOWN.
I THOUGHT I'D SLAIN YOU WHEN LAST WE MET.
ME? NO. I'M STILL ALIVE.
AND PORTHOS, HOW'S HE DOING?
CLONK
CLINK
CLINK
CLANK

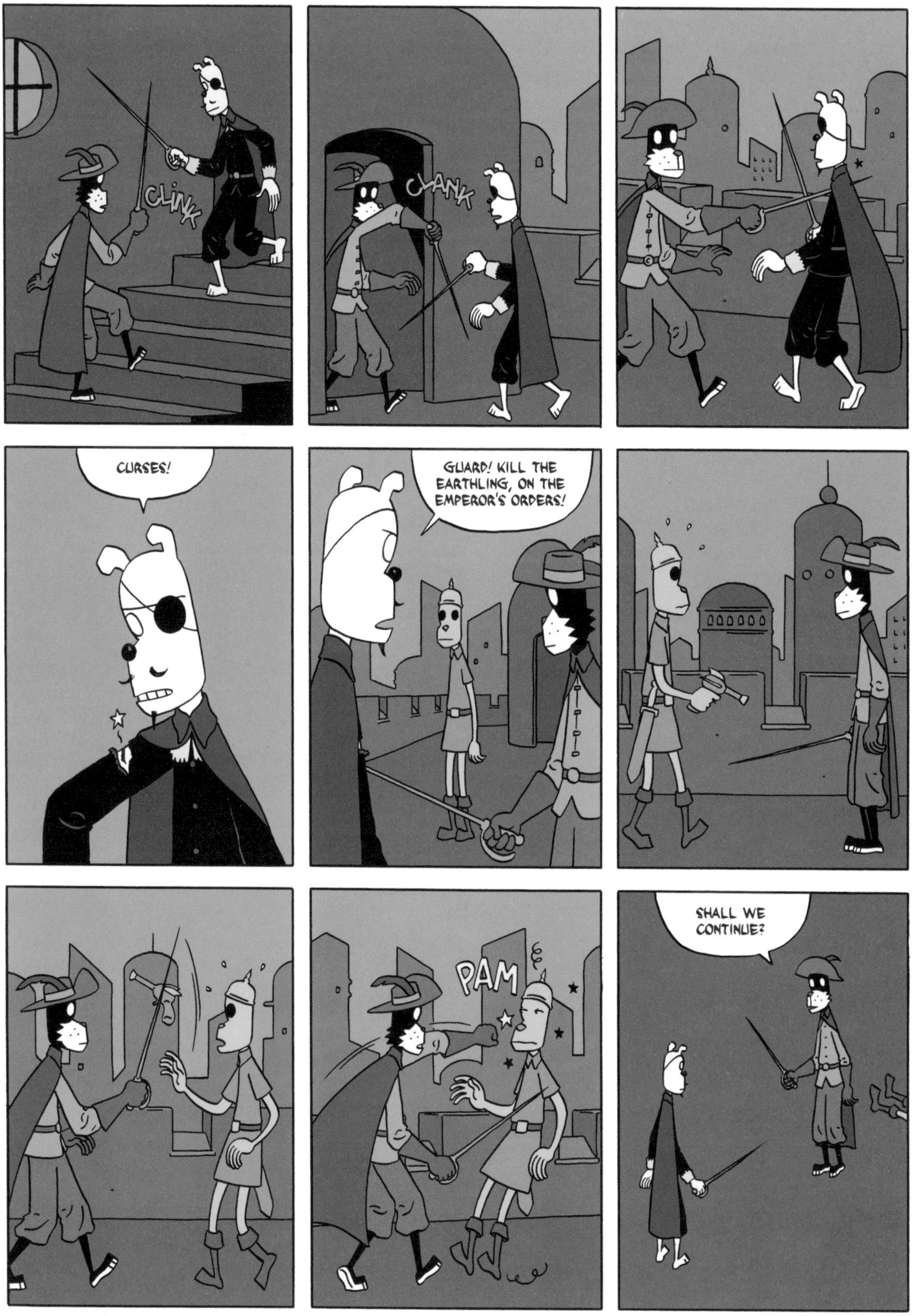
CLINK
CLANK
CURSES!
GUARD! KILL THE EARTHLING, ON THE EMPEROR'S ORDERS!
PAM
SHALL WE CONTINUE?

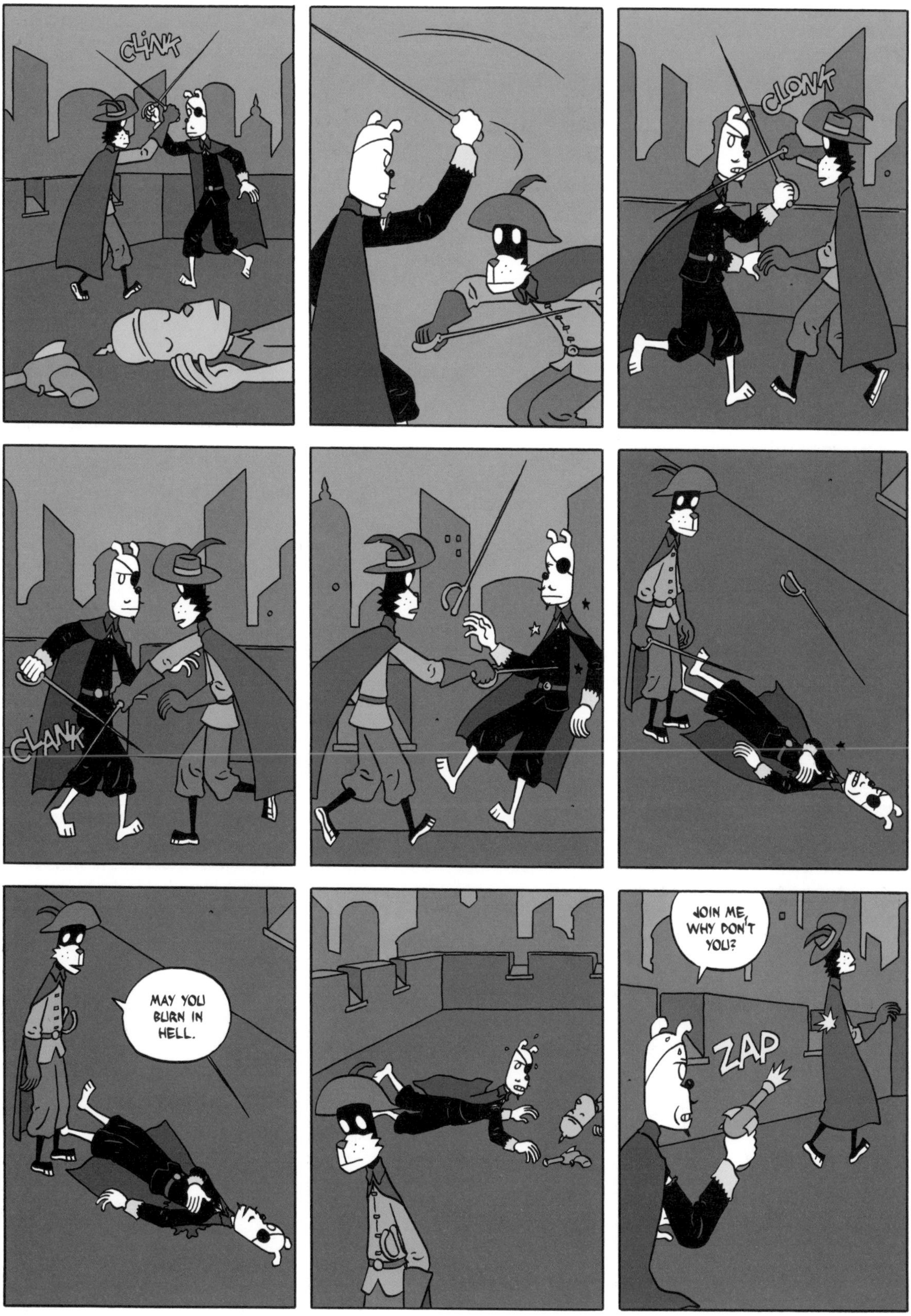
CLINK
CLONK
CLANK
MAY YOU BURN IN HELL.
JOIN ME, WHY DON'T YOU?
ZAP

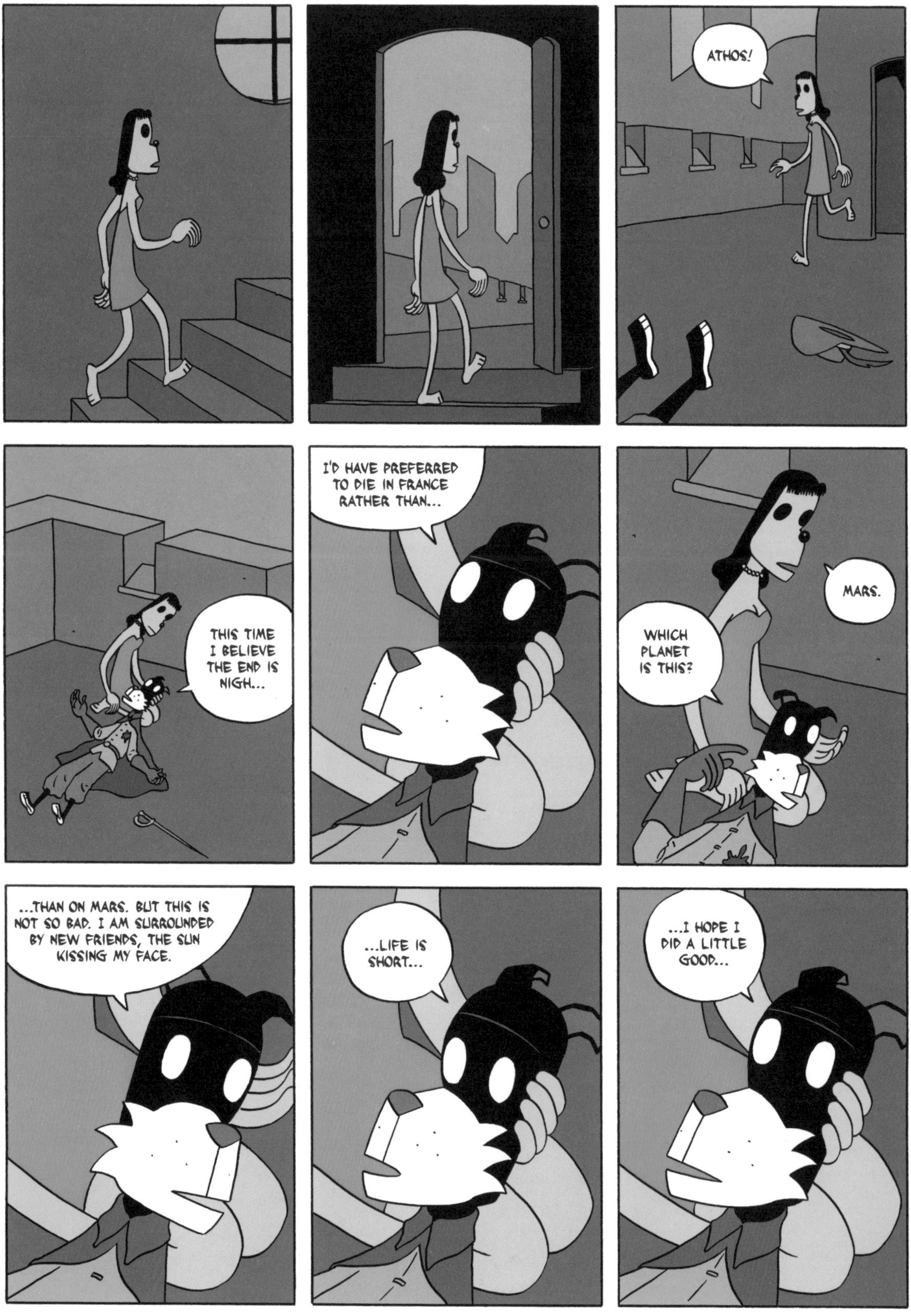
ATHOS!
THIS TIME I BELIEVE THE END IS NIGH...
I'D HAVE PREFERRED TO DIE IN FRANCE RATHER THAN...
WHICH PLANET IS THIS?
MARS.
...THAN ON MARS. BUT THIS IS NOT SO BAD. I AM SURROUNDED BY NEW FRIENDS, THE SUN KISSING MY FACE.
...LIFE IS SHORT...
...I HOPE I DID A LITTLE GOOD...

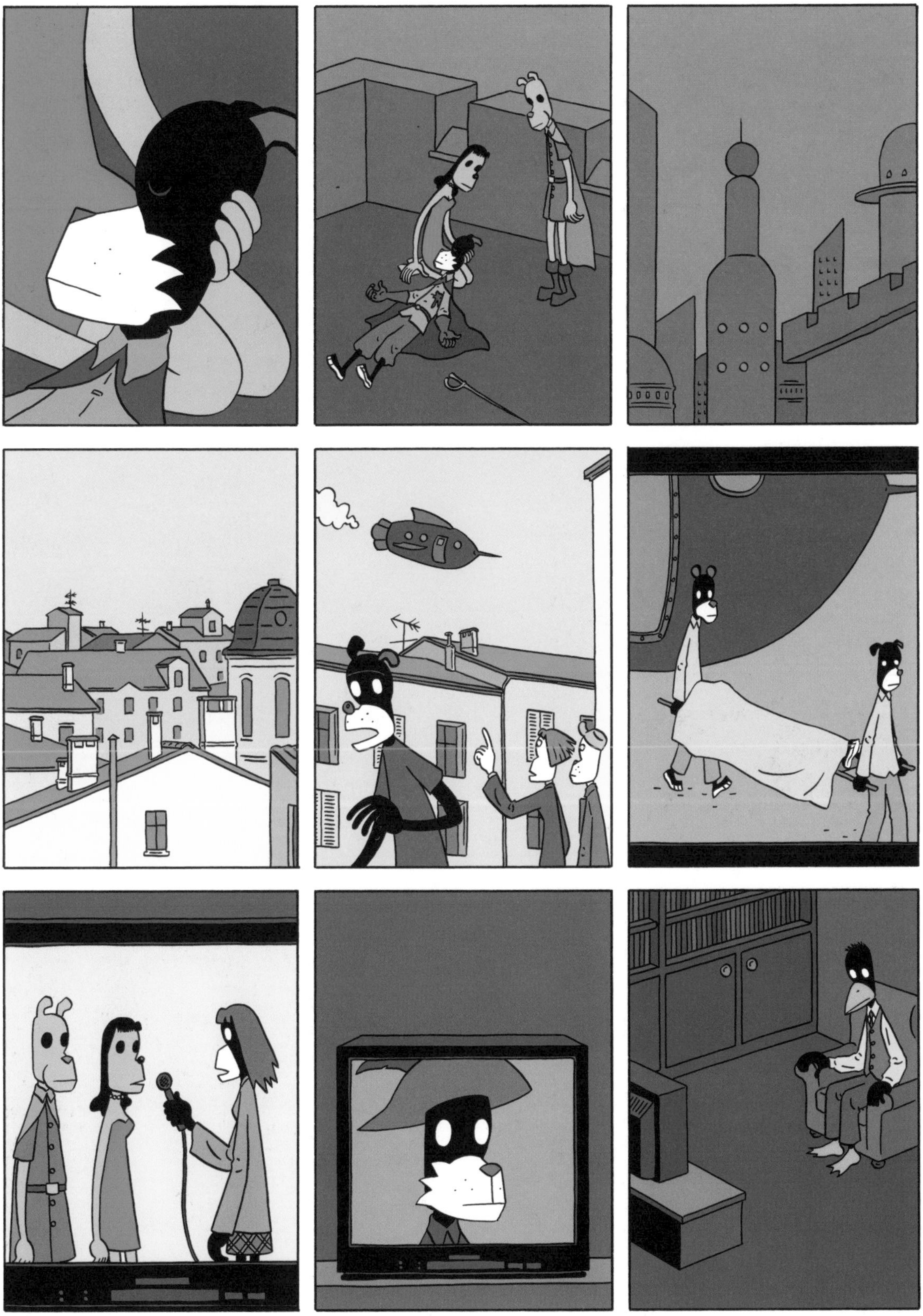

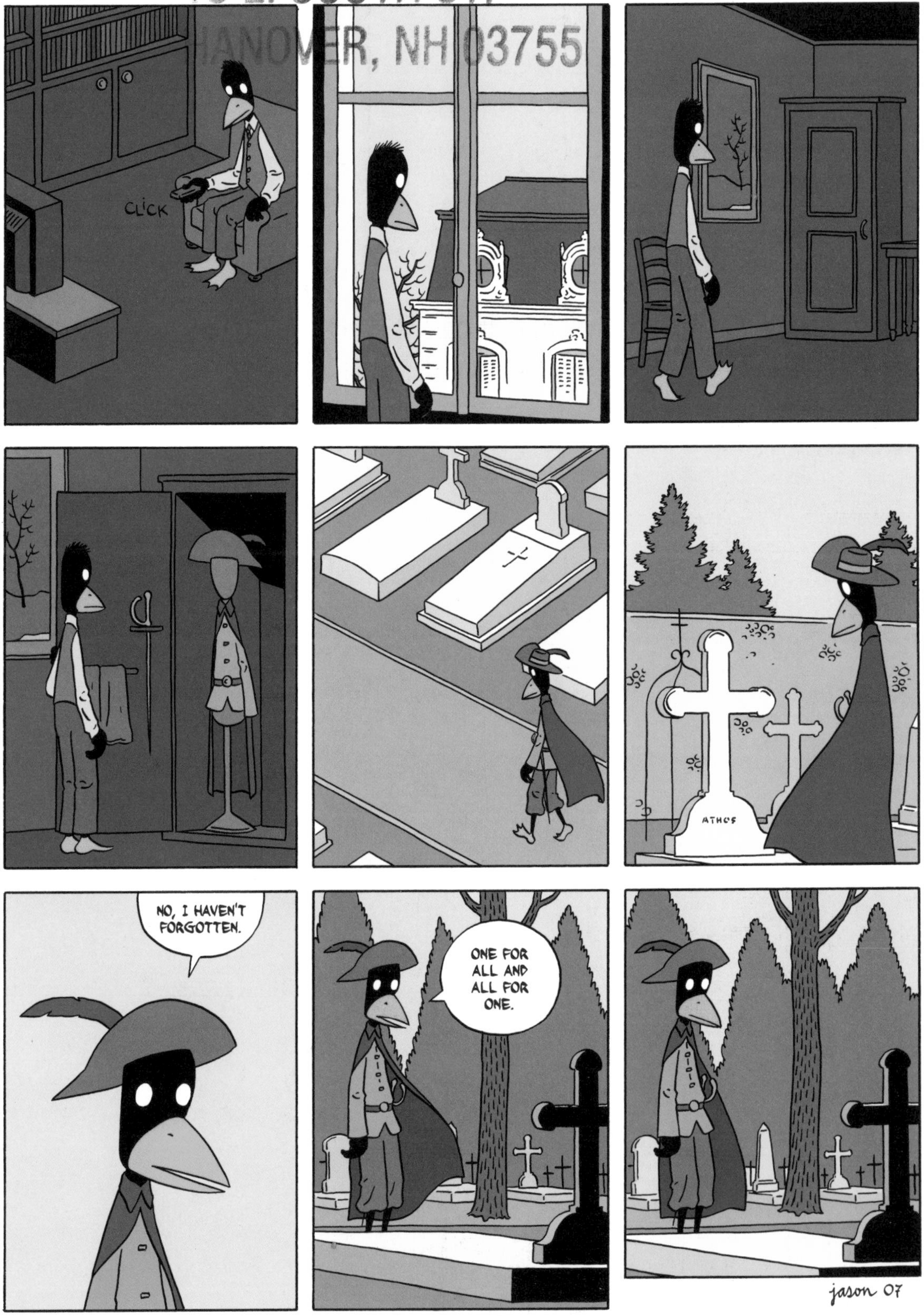
CLICK
ATHOS
NO, I HAVEN'T FORGOTTEN.
ONE FOR ALL AND ALL FOR ONE.
jason 07